The Bride's Book

The Bride's Book

A Pictorial History of American Bridal Dress

Catherine S. Zimmerman

ARBOR HOUSE
New York

Designed by Richard Oriolo

33013

Manufactured in the United States of America

10 9 8 7 6 5 4 3 2 1

This book is printed on acid free paper. The paper in this book meets the guidelines for permanence
and durability of the Committee on Production Guidelines for Book Longevity of the
Council on Library Resources.

Library of Congress Cataloging in Publication Data

Zimmerman, Catherine S.
The bride's book.

1. Wedding costume—United States—History.
I. Title.
GT1753.U6Z56   1985   391'.8   85-3877
ISBN 0-87795-704-5

Acknowledgments

For help in my initial research I would like to give special thanks to Julia S. Berrall, Upper Montclair, New Jersey, and to Elizabeth Ann Coleman of the Brooklyn Museum. Thanks also to Jane Stimmel and Nancy Wilson, proofreaders, and to the following people, who were helpful in my research:

Ruth Ann Clark, of the Historical Society of Delaware; Jean L. Druesedow, of the Metropolitan Museum of Art, New York; Pattilou Cobb, Texas Fashion Collection of North Texas State University; Patricia L. Collins, of the Harris County Heritage Society, Houston; Barbara Fisher, of the University of Texas at Austin; Ruth Hagy, of the Chester County Historical Society, Pennsylvania; Jean Hildreth, of the Arizona Costume Institute, Phoenix; Karlyn Istvan, Fort Washington, Maryland; Betty J. Mills, of the Texas Tech University, Lubbock; Joanne Olean, of the Museum of the City of New York; Louise E. Shaw and Elaine Kirkland of the Atlanta Historical Society; Carolyn T. Stewart of the University of Alabama; Anne Swanson, of Boston; Beatrice Taylor, of Winterthur Library, Winterthur, Delaware; and June L. Zimmerman, of Waldorf, Maryland.

My deepest thanks are extended to my husband, Dr. W. Russell Zimmerman, whose support and understanding throughout the long years of research helped to make this book a reality.

CATHERINE SHEPLEY ZIMMERMAN

Contents

Part I

Early America

1

The New World Bride: Daughters of the Native American, the Puritan, the Farmer, Planter, and Statesman (1500-1700)

What celebration compares to a wedding? If we were to look down at the American landscape from high above, we would see a never-ending procession of joyful men and women walking down the aisles toward matrimony. What party could match nearly five hundred years of colorful pageantry from all the cultures that make up our country? And what element of the celebration catches our eye and our imagination more than how the bride looks and what she is wearing?

Come with me on a delightful trip down the aisles from the early years of our country's history right up until today. Whether you're preparing for a wedding yourself or are simply going to sit in the audience, a look at the changing fashions of the American bride will bring the ceremony to you as surely as if you were hearing the vows yourself.

Native Americans

At the head of the parade of celebrants is the original American bride, the native Indian woman.

Close to the year 1000, explorers first made their way to our continent. Since the land was inhabited by a people with no disposition to buy and nothing at all to sell (save furs and game), the mariners moved on. Hearing tales of travels to the new land, women were reluctant to face the wilderness and had no desire to become part of the explorers' lives in the distant world.

What the early visitors missed was a beautiful expanse of land populated with a diverse nation of strong, peaceful people. Their ways were simple, their needs and desires satisfied by a life of basic outdoor living.

ILLUSTRATION 2. *Unmarried Hopi and Zuni women coiled their hair in large whorls over each ear (symbolizing the squash blossom), to designate marriageable status.*

ILLUSTRATION 1. *In a painting called* The Wedding, *by Eanger Irving Couse, a young brave shares his blanket with the chosen girl who would be his wife.*

One thing unknown to Indian culture was cloth. There was no cotton, wool, or silk. For centuries, animals skins sufficed for clothing for the eastern tribes, and from years of experience in preparing them came beautiful, extremely soft garments.

What of the young bride of the eastern nation called the Delawares, or Lenni-Lenapes? For her there was no formal marriage ceremony, no nuptial vow; her parents might have arranged a union with a chosen partner, but more often than not, a young couple merely decided to live together as man and wife.

The Indian girl who reached puberty was honored and elaborately fêted with ceremonials, dances, and celebrations. Then the news was spread that she was of marriageable age. As the galas ended, the date might be chosen and a marriage performed. Unlike the puberty festivals, if a marriage took place, it was a simple, casual affair. Sometimes an exchange of gifts could make up the entire ceremony. And the gifts—jewelry,

ILLUSTRATION 3.

blankets, a belt of wampum—were given not to the woman a young man was courting, but to her parents. If the parents accepted the gifts, the union was accepted.

What would a young Indian bride wear on that special day? Probably a new knee-length skirt of deerskin and a band of wampum beads around her forehead. Her body would be bare from the waist up, except for fine stone beads or shell necklaces for decoration. (Gold, silver, precious stones, and glass were unknown to her culture.) Her hair—her pride—would be long, sleek, and shiny black, dressed with bear grease. In cold weather, the young bride would wear deerskin leggings and moccasins and a robe of turkey feathers smooth as down.

Fashion was essentially unknown to this free spirit. True, she did paint her face and body; painting the face with white, red, and yellow clay was a favorite custom. White was a symbol of happiness and peace. (See Chapter 4, page 48.) Red was a favored color; Indian women reddened their eyelids, dabbed circular red spots on their cheeks, and sometimes outlined the rims of their ears in red. Tattoos were also worn, by both men and women. A bird, an animal, or a plant was scraped with a sharp bone or flint and powered tree bark or paint was rubbed into the design.[1]

Public displays of affection were shunned by the Indians, regardless of tribe. Romantic love and tenderness were very private and were kept under control—even hidden. Some tribes regarded passion and sentimentality as something to be pitied—a type of mental illusion that brought emotions to the surface and swept away any reasonable existence. The Indians did not

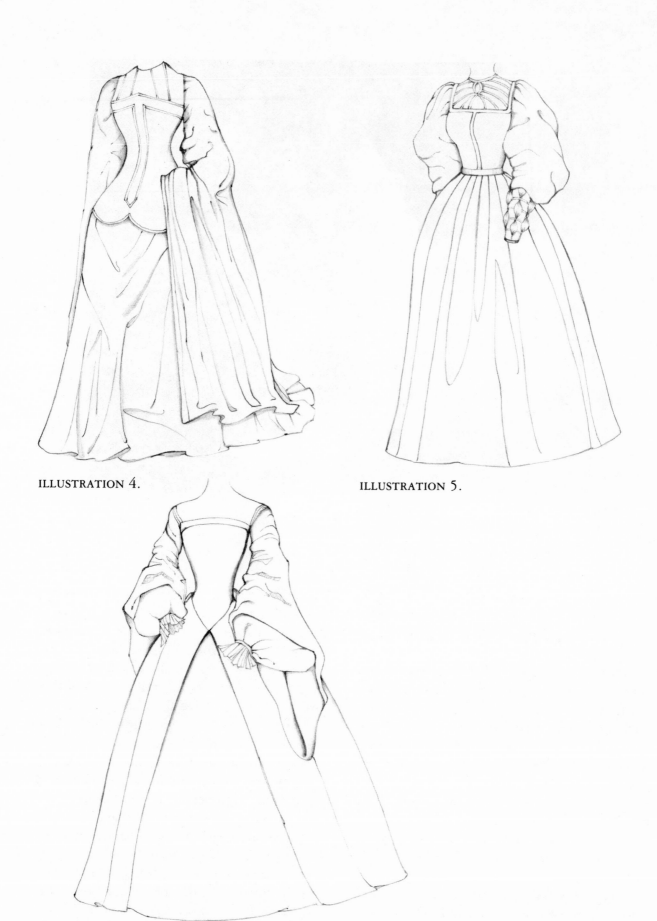

ILLUSTRATION 4.

ILLUSTRATION 5.

ILLUSTRATION 6.

ILLUSTRATION 7.

ILLUSTRATION 8. *English, c. 1540–54.*

kiss—at least never in public. But affection was very real, and marriages were usually strong and enduring.

Before the white men came, the Pueblos raised cotton (among other agricultural crops) and the women wore cotton garments. (This was not found among the eastern tribes.) The garments went beneath the left shoulder, were tied above the right shoulder, and were further secured by a belt around the waist.

In Navajo culture, women were strong and influential. Clans were matrilineal—women owned crops, houses, and furnishings. They were also important in political, religious, and social life. A bride was an equal partner with her husband.

Feasting made up the entire Navajo marriage ceremony. The Navajo bride and groom ate maize pudding together. There was no known wedding dance.

Illustration 3 shows the continuing traditional dress for literally hundreds of years without change. In the picture album in which it was found, it was captioned "Pansy, in Wedding Costume." She was Pansy Wawxnim, a Hopi Indian living in Oraibi, age about nineteen or twenty. She married Jim Kewanwytewa, age twenty-four or twenty-five, on October 25, 1919.

There are a few deviations in this twentieth-century Indian costume. For example, the bride did not wear her hair in the old ceremonial fash-

ILLUSTRATION 9. *A style of ruff, mid-sixteenth century.*

ion. Perhaps hers was a Christian nuptial ceremony performed by a priest, or she may even have been marrying for the second time.

European Settlers

After the discovery of the New World, all of Europe scrambled to acquire land and find riches. The High Renaissance in Europe was a time of bold contrasts. The nobility and the wealthy wore elegant fabrics, rich laces, silks and satins, in flamboyant styles; the poor lived in truly deplor-

able conditions. The situation on American shores was equally primitive. Yet colonizing America came slowly.

Spain was the first to claim her American empire. For most of the sixteenth century, Spaniards came to discover, trade, hunt, and possess. Eventually explorers' wives braved the long, dangerous sea journey to live in the new land as well.

The white-skinned women who arrived, clothed in colorful, soft fabric, must have seemed quite a strange sight to their Indian sisters. The women who came to the New World preserved their own culture, bringing favorite household items and raw materials for future use. We can easily imagine a bit of fine fabric brought along for a future wedding dress.

The Spanish settled in the West Indies, Central America, Mexico, and eventually Southern California. In 1540, near the Rio Grande, Spanish explorers first discovered the Pueblos people. The vast territories the Spanish conquered became known as New Spain. The Spanish women brought along handsome silks, rich leathers, and choice laces to wear in their new homes. Determined to live genteelly, they resisted the primitive life of the new country. As Spain encouraged her colonies to be dependent on the homeland, private enterprise was discouraged. Everything was imported, carrying the image of luxury to American shores.

Spain was not the only country whose emigrants were determined to preserve their own culture. Natives of each European nation longed to propagate the kind of life known in the mother country.

More transplanting was done than planting. Many young couples felt it was wiser to marry in the original homeland, for little or nothing in the way of finished goods was available after the Atlantic crossing was made.

ILLUSTRATION 10. *A contemporary woodcut (1982) of Anne Burroughs's wedding dress.*

ILLUSTRATION 11.

As princesses married nobles of neighboring European countries, cultures and women's clothing meshed in the 1500s and 1600s. The styles of each individual country were retained with small details of ornamentation.

Illustrations 4 and 5 show the general cut and outline of dresses. Illustration 4 is Spanish in origin, c. 1501, the style worn by Catherine of Aragon, daughter of Ferdinand and Isabella, who became the first wife of Henry VIII of England in 1509.

Illustration 5 is also Spanish, c. 1503–1508. The wealthier a woman was, the richer the fabric she wore, and the more gold, silver, and precious jewels ornamented it. Long trains worn in Europe did not succeed in America. The bride who married in the New World brought along enough material for her dress to style it in the prevailing fashion, but her entire creation was much simpler.

Illustration 6 is an English style, dated around 1546. The neckline remained common, and basi-

ILLUSTRATION 12.

cally the style survived until the mid-1600s, with
an overskirt, long pointed bodice, long over-
sleeves, and tight undersleeves. Pushing the skirt
out was a popular fashion accessory, the farthingale: a flat, wide hoopskirt of felt or horsehair
(later made of metal hoops or whalebone). Padding and bolstering were often needed to accommodate it. The wheel farthingale appeared at the
end of the reign of Elizabeth I. In the colonies
padding sufficed, and the farthingale disappeared.

The dress of Lady Jane Gray, portrayed in a
steel engraving (Ill. 7), shows a slightly less rigid
style, not overly laden with jewels or lace. Lady
Jane Gray, great-granddaughter of Henry VII,
was Queen of England for only nine days.

Dutch women who came to the New World
brought supplies of cut garments with them. In

New Amsterdam the Dutch women wore color-
ful, short, full petticoats, scarlet or green, striped
with black or gray. Aprons were indispensable. A
bride, too, might have worn a pretty apron, with
modest decorative edging and a girdle with ribbon or silver chain suspended from it. With a cap
of dainty muslin and lace and a plain ruff, it was
an attractive bridal costume.

The Dutch were especially fond of the ruff, a
rigid and high-standing collar, usually made of
lace. It could be stiffened with rice water or fluted
and propped up with wire or pasteboard, then
starched into elaborate pleating. Queen Elizabeth
took the fashion to its extreme. (In England, it
was called the Tudor ruff.) The Spanish, too,
used the ruff extensively. It reached its greatest
popularity by 1620 in Europe. When it became
old-fashioned, the Puritans adopted it in
simplified form; thus in America it became the
mark of the strict follower.

Tall ships continued to ply the waters of the
Atlantic as the sixteenth century drew to a close,
supplying those commodities so desired for wedding apparel. England's early settlers kept close
ties with the home country, doing their best to
carry abroad the fashion and quality of living
familiar to them. Settlers in Virginia still faced
grave dangers. Soon after he had arrived in the
colony of Roanoke, Governor John White was
urged to sail back to England for much needed
supplies. Three years later he returned to America
to find that all the colonists (including his daughter) had disappeared without a trace, leaving behind no explanation of their fate.

The first successful settlement was in James-
town, Virginia. Under King James I, a ship was
fitted out with 105 colonists. After five months it
arrived on the James River on May 13, 1607.

The first English wedding in the New World

ILLUSTRATIONS 13, 14, &
15. *Early wedding garb in the
colonies is clearly portrayed in
these illustrations.*

took place in 1608 in Virginia between John Laydon and Anne Burroughs. Captain John Smith, president of Virginia, recorded the wedding, along with his account of arriving settlers:

2 appointed to Council
Master Francis West, brother to the
    Lord La Warre
22 Gentlemen,   11 Tradesmen
18 Laborers   2 Boys
and Mistress Forrest and her maid
8 Dutchmen and Poles,   70 persons
                        in all[2]

Among this group of arrivals were the first English women to come to Virginia, Mrs. Forrest and her maid, Anne Burroughs. It was the maid, Anne, who became the first English bride to be married on American soil.

Illustration 11 represents the style of dress worn by the maid. It was of similar cut to Mrs. Forrest's, but was of linsey-woolsey (a coarse woolen material first made at Linsey, in Suffolk, England), with cuffs and falling band (a large collar) of plain linen. The costume has an overskirt opening over a petticoat. It also has a stiffened ruff around the neck. A modified farthingale supports the dress, which hangs in heavy plaits to the ground. The trimming on the bodice is of silk galloon (a kind of lace made of silk, often woven with cotton, gold, or silver), with a design in gold thread. The close-fitting cap (or coif) of white linen is shaped over the ruff in the back.[3]

The Puritans

The first wedding celebrated among the settlers who laid the foundation of Boston was between

ILLUSTRATION 16.

two young lovers who met in England when they were eighteen. Oliver Temple's parents were loyal orthodox defenders of the royal prerogative and surpliced priests of the church. Rebecca Welden was a nonconformist who saw her parents die for their religious beliefs. Realizing the persecution his fiancée had faced, Oliver became a convert to the creed of the nonconforming Puritans. When he asked his father for permission to marry Rebecca, making clear his new faith, his father denounced the engagement and the young pair separated.

Oliver's father sent him to London in hopes of returning him to the fold. Instead, the young man spent all his energy searching for Rebecca. At last he was told that both Rebecca and her brother were dead, Rebecca of a fever and her brother by his own hand. Undaunted, Oliver secretly boarded a ship of Puritans bound for America in the spring of 1630.

ILLUSTRATION 17.

During the two months' confinement on the sailing vessel, the friends Oliver made tried to promote a match with a young woman, to no avail. At last the long voyage came to an end, and the ship pulled into the harbor of Salem. Who should be waiting to greet Oliver but the long-lost brother of his fiancée! It seemed that Oliver's father had made up the story of the two deaths to insure that his son never marry a girl of the Puritan faith.

On July 8, 1630, a day of rejoicing, Oliver Temple and Rebecca Welden were married.[4] There is no description of what Rebecca wore on that happy wedding day, but the story puts her in the company of the Puritan women of Massachusetts in the earliest colonizations there, and we *do* know what these women wore. Illustration 13 is most likely a good approximation of what Rebecca wore on that day.

The Pilgrims were content to retain the English style of dress, but they simplified the ornamentation, discarding ribbons, lace, feathers, and costly textiles. They even made laws regulating the cut of boots, sleeves, and hoods and the amount of money a person could spend on a wardrobe.

Since the Puritans admired industriousness, work clothes were viewed with approval. The Puritan woman wore a gown with a close bodice, a full skirt of camlet (a combination of wool and silk), looped back over a petticoat of homespun. Colors were green, brown, or dull purple. Neckerchiefs were tucked into the bodice top, and the women proudly displayed their freshly laundered aprons of snowy white linen. Turned-back cuffs ornamented the sleeves. There were caps of a variety of shapes of muslin or lace, which allowed very little of the hair to show. Hair was parted in the middle and drawn back closely. Hoods of dark colors were worn out-of-doors, and sometimes a broad-brimmed Pilgrim hat, as in Illustration 12.

One would imagine the Boston Puritan or Plymouth Pilgrim bride would wear somber black and white, with a white whisk collar, black bodice, white apron, and broad-brimmed black hat. Some Puritan women did dress this way, but most brides chose a lovely color and becoming style, still following the required restraints.

Oddly, early Puritan ministers were not allowed to perform marriages, despite their powerful influence in every other aspect of their culture.

Instead, ruling magistrates, squires, tavernkeepers, and captains could marry Puritan lovers. In fact, practically any man of dignity or prominence in the community could receive authority to perform that rite—except the parson![5]

The Quakers

As the influx of English-speaking peoples continued, the colonies on the east coast of America gained a secure footing. In 1680, on the banks of the Delaware, William Penn established a free state founded on the principle of universal brotherhood. Like other Protestants in Europe's brutal years of war, the Friends had been buffeted with shameful persecutions, imprisonment, and exile, and now their hopes lay in America.

The Quaker state of Pennsylvania was characterized by nonviolence and integrity. For over seventy years, Indians and Quakers kept a pledge of peace. Thus, within the borders of Pennsylvania, a Quaker hat and coat was a better defense than a military uniform and a musket.

Philadelphia's growth was astonishing. In the summer of 1683, there were only three or four houses. The ground squirrels lived in their burrows and wild deer ran through the town without alarm. Two years later, the city contained six hundred houses. The schoolmaster, preacher, and merchant had come and the printing press had begun its work.

Quaker dress has often been thought of as distinctive and set apart. Yet drab and gray and brown were not Quaker colors. At first, all Quaker women wore colored aprons of green or blue, preferably green. The quarterly meeting at Lincolnshire in 1721 said distinctly: "We think Green aprons are Decent and becoming to us as a People."[6]

A strong sense of decorum and modesty in the sincerity of their faith resulted in "plain dress"; but this simply meant unassuming apparel in the current styles of the day—minus all the extravagances. There were no hat bands, no needless buttons, buckles, etc. There was no standard of perfect plainness, but the early Quaker rule stated that every article from head to foot should exhibit this plainness, and it applied to everyone.

The earliest Quaker women wore hoods, known as cardinals, riding hoods, or capuchins. It was from this early dress, worn around Philadelphia until about 1880, that most of us get the idea of Quaker clothing: soft gray bonnet, dress, shawl, sheer cap worn under the bonnet, and white scarf worn around the throat, or sometimes tucked in at the waist.[7] The shawl, worn in different ways, was also known as a handkerchief, a fichu, or whisk. Yet Quakers stopped wearing this garb when it began to attract too much attention, although even today they avoid showy colors and prefer conservative styles. (See Illus. 28 and 29, depicting eighteenth-century Quaker wedding dresses.)

In Illustration 16, we see what a young bride wore in the early Dutch town on Manhattan Island, the capital of New Netherland (renamed New York by the British in 1664).

One woman, Catalina Trico, came to New Netherland with the first expedition sent there by the West India Company. She told of her experiences aboard ship, when four women were married at sea. The four couples stayed in New Netherland only three weeks, then, by order of the Dutch governor, settled along the Delaware River.[8]

For brides of the New World's first two hundred years, wedding dresses were not considered finery, to be put away for posterity; they are not the gowns that end up in our museums. These dresses were worn until they were threadbare. Any excess material left over from making them was used in coverlets or quilts. Colonial women concentrated on homemaking and survival in the wilderness, and so didn't think to save and preserve clothes for the good of history. As few examples remain, we know what brides wore only from journals, letters, and diaries. Good descriptions of wedding dresses can be found scattered throughout historical society archives and museums across America, and in family archival possessions.

The word to describe culture in these early years is *varied*. The bride daughter of the southern plantation owner lived an unhurried life in a beautifully furnished home in the late 1600s. She could wear the best of English linen and wool, or French silks. The stern New England or Pennsylvania farmer's daughter would be wedded in a much simpler dress. The daughter of a Boston statesman would wear brocades and rich fabrics from England.

Illustration 17 shows the style of dress worn in the last half of the seventeenth century; it is of English and Dutch origin. A decorative apron was worn with it. Women were proud of the number of petticoats of rich materials they owned. These demanded a professional handling of the folds; the skirt was looped up and pinned back, or raised to a necessary height to avoid being dragged through a puddle.

Our first panoramic view of the New World bride has spanned two hundred years, up to 1700. These beginnings in America for many young women who were brides of the settlers can be likened to transplanting a seedling, then watching it grow and flourish in a distant location. These daughters of Puritan, farmer, planter, and statesman present the picture of the early joyous procession of brides in America.

2

Brocade to
Linsey-Woolsey (1700-1750)

Numbers can be very precise; history is not so neat. The first day of a new century does not signal a completely fresh start; history is a continuous thread. Many parallel strands interweave those of another direction, creating a fabric—a true picture, as on a tapestry. The same is true for clothing.

For the first quarter of the eighteenth century, Europe neatly categorized classes of people. The period of the Grand Monarchy, the reign of Louis XIV of France, lasted for seventy-two years (1643–1714). During this time, France set the style for the rest of the world. The court modes were extreme and ostentatious; women's clothes were made of luxurious, heavily ornamented brocades and silks. Even informal dresses had trains, which had to be carried by a lackey. Many

of the garments that found their way to the colonies in sea chests and packing boxes contained some handsome silks and brocades. Family heirlooms (especially those in New England and the South) testify to the fact that the sumptuous look and the feel of silk damask and brocade were prized. In the still-rugged America there was a need for special attention to dress, a preference for bright colors, and some extravagance of costume.

Illustration 18 shows the shape of gowns in Europe in the first part of the eighteenth century. The panier* was very popular and was made of stiffened linen; it increased in size until about

---

*A panier is a structure or device worn at the sides to extend the hips. It is also a portion of a skirt arranged to provide fullness at the sides.

ILLUSTRATION 18.

1730, when it measured six feet in diameter. The paniers led to many silhouette changes.

Around 1736 dresses took on a graceful line that adapted very well to the paniers. Being trapezoidal in shape, the entire sleeve fitted to the arms, ending in rich volants of lace at the elbows. This silhouette inspired Yves St. Laurent to design the modern "trapeze" dress in 1957.

The colonial woman knew that her life-style was not like court life; nor did it include a great deal of the rich formality found in baroque Europe. Although New World hardships were decreasing and conditions were steadily improving, early Americans had to wear a certain amount of homespun and homemade clothes. In the colonies linsey-woolsey was a practical material. Its wool and linen content provided warmth for the cold winters.

For early America, the idea of a melting pot would have appalled transplanted natives of European countries. Each wanted to colonize part of the vast new land and make it an extension of his or her homeland in Europe. The Germans were the last Europeans to come to America in this period, and they were no exception to this rule. The peace-loving German Baptist Brethren (or Dunkers) and the Mennonites, at the hospitable invitation of William Penn, settled at first in

ILLUSTRATION 19.

ILLUSTRATION 20. *Style of dress worn in Germany in the seventeenth and early eighteenth century.*

ILLUSTRATION 21.

Germantown (1683–1729) and later in other parts of the Commonwealth of Pennsylvania. Coming from the low countries along the Rhine, they found Pennsylvania much like the homeland they had left; the rich resources of productive land, abundant food, and good climate aided them in establishing substantial homes. They preserved their culture's nationalism, and an active family life centered around religious devotion.

One general style of dress was worn by both German and Austrian women. As seen in Illustration 21, the skirts were full and not always long.

The bodices were dark and were laced over coarse white shifts. The "plain" people, as these Germans came to be called, were a religious folk. A genuine humility pervaded their daily lives. Having no desire to be "worldly," fashion was far from their minds. Content to be farmers—and they became extremely proficient at this—their dress was not picturesque and surely not "fashionable." In fact, these country women adopted a dress much like that of the Quakers; of very simple cut, it was plain drab,* black or brown in

*Drab is a dull-colored fabric made of thick wool or cotton.

There existed in colony, province, and state, certainly for over two hundred years, a simple, neighborly, homely custom known as "Coming out Bride". This one very pleasing interruption...no, I cannot call it by so severe a name, ... one very pleasing diversion of the attention of the congregation from the parson was caused by the innocent custom that prevailed in many a country community. Just fancy the flurry on a June Sabbath in Killingly, in 1785, when Joseph Gay, clad in a velvet coat, lace-frilled shirt, and white broadcloth knee-breeches, with his fair bride of a few days, gorgeous in a peach-coloured silk gown and a bonnet trimmed with sixteen yards of white ribbon, rose, in the middle of the sermon from their front seat in the gallery and stood for several minutes, slowly turning around in order to show from every point of view their bridal finery to the eagerly gazing congregation of friends and neighbors. Such was the really delightful and thoughtful custom, in those fashion-plateless days, among persons of wealth in that and other churches.....It was, in fact, part of the wedding celebration. Even in mid-winter, in the icy church, the blushing bride would throw aside her broadcloth cape or camblet roquelo and stand up, clad in a sprigged India muslin gown with only a thin lace tucker over her neck, warm with pride in her pretty gown, her white bonnet with ostrich feathers and embroidered veil, and in her new husband.

Alice Morse Earle

ILLUSTRATION 22.

ILLUSTRATION 23. *The brocade design.*

ILLUSTRATIONS 24 & 25. *These two illustrations show the style of the dress only, in front and back views. They do not accurately portray an eighteenth-century gown; it was greatly altered in the mid-1800s. The entire costume includes a petticoat of rose-pink quilted silk.*

color. Buckles and buttons were condemned, as were laces, silks and satins, trimmings, etc.

The Mennonites and Amish were known as "Hookers," from the hooks and eyes that fastened their clothes. Their simple American dress was free from the overdressing of the times: the powdered wigs, ornate headdresses, flounces, fringes, stomachers (false fronts or ornamental coverings on front of the bodice), and all the excesses of costly court dress. Instead, their clothing was distinctive in character; their homemade cloth, woven from tow (flax, hemp, or jute fiber prepared for spinning), was made from flax grown on virgin soil. Garments were made to last a long time without a change in style. Quaint caps, known as prayer caps, were small and worn close to the head with bonnets over them. Most Amish and some Mennonite women still wear this type of cap today.

The dress of the Dunkers (or Dunkards) was so uniform that all clothes were made from the same pattern, the distinguishing feature of which was a dainty kerchief of the same material as the dress. This kerchief was worn over the shoulders, with the long points extending to the waist in the front and back. The headdress was the characteristic bonnet—plain, unadorned, white, and covering the entire head, extending beyond the face and tied under the chin.

The Pennsylvania Germans are popularly known as the Pennsylvania Dutch, a corruption of the German word *Deutsch,* meaning "German." A bride of the Pennsylvania Germans naturally followed the prototype of her ancestors. Months of planning and painstaking detail went into the sewing of a wedding dress and trousseau. Examples of wedding clothes, including undergarments, can be found today. They show beautiful handiwork in fine stitches, hemstitching, tuck-

ing, and white embroidery. Women of some groups wore large aprons that covered them entirely in front and extended down the back as far as the girdle.

In some respects, certain segments of the Pennsylvania Germans set up very strict laws and lived by them. Today, unburdened by such constricting social edicts, we are shocked that such conditions existed among the Germans in America. According to one account of the period (c. 1749), before laws were made to protect the rights of a married woman, she could hold no property individually; after her husband's death she did not even have legal ownership of her own clothes, unless they were bequeathed to her. The clothes on her back belonged to the estate of her husband!

If the widow remarried, care had to be taken that the first husband's affairs were in no way involved with the second husband's. To insure this, it was necessary for the woman to be married in nothing but her shift (underclothing), for she had to release her clothes to the first husband's estate. This freed her from any claims. After the ceremony she was given clothing by her new husband.[9] In a transaction that took place in New Jersey in 1749, one woman went out of the house of her deceased husband to that of her bridegroom in nothing but her shift. The groom met her halfway with fine new clothes, telling all who were present that he lent them to his bride. Then he put them on her with his own hands. His reason for saying that he lent the clothes rather than gave them as a gift was so the creditors could not take them before she was again a married woman.[10]

This extreme example, however, is quite isolated from the usual practice of wedding ceremonies among the Germans. Joyous celebrations

ILLUSTRATION 26.

were given nearly everyone, from farmers' daughters to those in small towns. The German Lutherans had no laws concerning the restricting of dress styles.

Descriptions of weddings, unfortunately, have more to say about customs and food than the bride's dress. Still, we can read about one farmer's daughter who awaited her groom at six o'clock on an October morning dressed in a purple mousseline-de-laine dress and a blue bonnet. The

Amish weddings were not held in churches, but in private homes. No one went to these wedding but invited guests, and perhaps one or two very intimate "outside" (non-Amish) friends.

In the rich, fertile farmland of Amish country, particularly in Pennsylvania, after the growing season and harvest, young Amish couples looked forward to the wedding season. Pantry shelves and cellars were filled with the season's preserved foods.

groom had eaten, fed and harnessed the horses, attired himself, and ridden four miles. After the wedding the bride and groom rode to Lancaster by horse and buggy, later in the afternoon to Philadelphia. Receptions, or homecomings, were given to them when they returned home.[11]

There was food of all kinds in abundance for the November wedding of Rachel Zook and Levi Fisher. By 8:00 A.M. on the wedding day, the Zook farmyard was already cluttered with gray boxlike family buggies and the black open buggies of the young men. The ground floor of the old stone house had been cleared of its furniture to make room for twenty or more benches and chairs. At exactly nine o'clock, the wedding party—the bride, her three attendants, called "waiters," the groom, and his three attendants—took their places on a front-row bench.

Rachel was dressed in a light blue, rather formless dress made by her mother. An ample, white organdy apron extended from waist to lower hem and two-thirds of the way around her body. Pinned to the top of the apron and extending snugly across her breast, over her shoulders, and down to the top of the apron in the back was a triangular white organdy *halstuch* (neckerchief). Symbolic of the constancy of her wedding vows was the fact that she would never again wear her bridal apron and *halstuch* until she died. No rings were worn; in fact, not a woman in the entire room, whether in the bridal party or in the congregation, wore cosmetics, jewelry, or flowers.

There was no instrumental music—only singing, intonations, sermons, and ritual—as the couple exchanged vows. Strong tradition dictated all aspects of Amish courtship and wedding practices. Yet there was a great deal of festivity, too. There still is, in fact, for Rachel and Levi's wedding took place in the 1970s, with the same

ritual as in the early 1700s.[12]

While happy weddings were being held in Pennsylvania and the Middle Atlantic colonies, with pretty young girls wearing homespun dresses and crisp white aprons, New England girls were being wed in imported brocades or silks and were following a delightful custom called "coming out bride."

Coming Out Bride

America was still provincial in the year 1700. Travel was very limited and it was difficult to find out what the latest trends in fashions were; women were starved for the views of current modes and styles from Europe. Fashion plates were still unknown in the colonies and the simple, neighborly custom known as "coming out bride" was practiced regularly. It was instructive and satisfying and occurred wherever it was possible to walk to church.

On the first Sunday after a wedding and usually for the four Sundays of the honeymoon month, bride and groom went to church services dressed in their wedding finery. They were attended by parents and friends, all walking together through narrow Boston streets to the Old South Meeting House. They did not take their usually assigned seats, but were seated in the most prominent place in the house, sometimes arriving a little late in order to gain attention. At a point in the service, the couple, alternating between shyness and pride, rose to their feet and slowly turned around two or three times before the eyes of the delighted assembly, displaying to the full every detail of their attire.

Many diaries are filled with references to "coming out bride." It was a common phrase in the northern colonies and remained a standard practice for well over a hundred years.

In 1719, one beautiful yellow silk brocade wedding gown with horizontal floral stripes was worn by Mary Leverett at her wedding in Cambridge, Massachusetts. The brocade introduced green, rose, light green and white in the silken stripe design. Later, it was worn to church for the coming out bride tradition.

Yellow and gold were favorite colors for bridal dresses in the 1700s. The heavy brocades that came from Europe often came in bolt form or yard goods; then the clothing was made up in the colonies. Gowns in blue brocade, and a few in pink and fawn, also exist.

Some intriguing true "coming out bride" stories from the early days of Boston and vicinity are found in the day's literature and history, as well as in personal diaries.

One proud little procession walked to the Old South Meeting House one Sunday morning, making a colorful party. Headed by the bride and groom, the others in attendance were the bride's parents and the bridal attendants. This event was important enough to a Boston judge that he recorded it in his diary. A generation later, the old judge again described the custom when his granddaughter wore her vast swaying hoop and brocade to church, smiling beneath her close cap and little hat. The groom was wearing a flowered velvet suit. In this bridal party the judge himself participated, looking somber in his black satin, his third wife in her striped Persian walking proudly behind him and the bridal pair.[13]

Later days continued the tradition of formality in the dress worn by those "coming out brides." Many elegant gowns were brought into public view. One seventeen-year-old bride was widowed only a few weeks after the wedding. Over ten years later, still young, she married a second time. For the "coming out bride" custom she wore a silver gray satin gown, and a gray pelisse* of uncut velvet with a silk stripe; this was lined with cherry-colored satin and trimmed with maribou plumes. Her bonnet was of shirred gray velvet with natural gray feathers and cherry-colored face trimmings of full ruches of ribbon loops. Etiquette did not approve of a widow's appearance in white bonnet, feathers, and veil, but this young widow felt that the gray bonnet made her seem like an old woman.

After another arm-in-arm procession to the church, one bride displayed her fawn-colored watered-silk gown and walked beside her proud husband, who was wearing the newest fashion—trousers.** These were made from the same piece of fawn-colored material as the gown.

A young Medford girl told of her sister's determination not to marry in April lest showers spoil her coming out. Although she waited until the last Sunday in May, a violent thunderstorm prevented her from going to church at all.[14] Until the time of analine dyes and synthetic fabrics, fine silks, brocades, damasks, and even linens could be permanently ruined by drops of water, moisture, perspiration or food oils.

Elizabeth Bull (daughter of a Boston merchant and tavern keeper) put her needlework skill to advantage in 1731 while she was still in school; later, in 1735, this beautiful silk with crewel embroidery was made up into her wedding dress. It was pale green silk, embroidered in crewel pattern with multicolored flowers.

For her September wedding in 1742, in Newburyport, Massachusetts (then called Newbury),

*A full-length coat or cloak of silk, wool or cotton, often fur-trimmed, sometimes fur-lined.
**Previously, men wore knee-breeches.

Mary Beck wore a gown of white taffeta, brocaded in a floral pattern with polychrome silks trimmed with self-ruchings. The young woman had to rely on fabrics and accessories brought from her home country. This particular silk brocade was woven at Spitalfields, England. The accessories included a quilted petticoat, a hat covered with polychrome feathers, green velvet shoes, and an ivory painted fan. A feature of note on this costume, as with many in these years, is the finished edges, which were pinked (not with the pinking shears we know today); although left raw, they never frayed. The style of dress was prevalent in the early eighteenth century: one-piece fitted bodice with low, square neck, elbow-length sleeves, which have the same pleated ruffle as the neckline. There are Engageant sleeves (sleeves with ruffles of sheer material, falling below the brocade sleeve). The overskirt had paniers, but in the American colonies the fullness of the side paniers was achieved by side pleating, not by stiffened linen or hoopskirt, as was the fashion in Europe. (The gown is in the costume collection of the Boston Museum of Fine Arts.)

In the late 1720s, a style of gown developed that remained a fashion favorite until about 1780: the sack or sack-back gown. A becoming style on any woman, the back had box pleats stitched down on each side of the back seam from the neckline to about shoulder level and then fell loosely to merge with the fullness of the skirt below. Sometimes it had a natural, fairly long train and gave the wearer a feeling of regal carriage. This style was also called the "Watteau pleat" gown (the artist Antoine Watteau often painted ladies wearing this type of dress). Brides, particularly, loved this fashion, as the flowing train afforded a built-in elegance.

A wedding dress worn in 1736 by Miss Jane Porter of Salem, Massachusetts, was of white brocaded silk. It had a handsome design of large baskets of red, blue, and raisin-colored blooms, with trailing green ferns and branches to link them. The gown had a loose sack-back, elbow-length sleeves, and a deeply scooped neckline.[15]

Bridal processions in the first half of the eighteenth century displayed elegant creations. Heavy silks, satins, and brocades literally swept from the shoulders into long trains. A bride gave a queenly appearance; her audience was captivated and delighted by the event.

At the same time, bridal clothing appeared in simple form. Linsey-woolsey or fresh cottons gave a special charm to the wearer. In this period, America was diverse, as always, in its fashion scene.

3

Pride of the Colonies:
The Graceful Age (1750-1800)

Bridal clothing worn by American brides in the mid-eighteenth century was picturesque and graceful. Women longed to know what was being worn in Europe, and the love of fashionable dress was marked throughout the colonies. Most often, it was the most extravagant styles that reached American shores. In Europe, rococo ornament had followed the more refined baroque style. Not quite as "busy" and ornamented as rococo art and architecture, fashions were less exuberant in America; thus some truly beautiful and graceful dresses were produced in the colonies.

Philadelphia grew into a stately, vibrant metropolis, and became an important colonial city, leading in many areas of cultural activity. Women of other cities, villages, and towns were aware of the fashions worn in Philadelphia. A large segment of Philadelphia's population was Quaker, and here, as in New England, some fine examples of wedding dresses worn by the Friends still exist.

Young Quaker women showed taste in their choice of dress. They also used the finest materials possible, knowing that garments made from them would last and retain good line and appearance. The attractive Quaker dresses that I have found argue the prevailing belief that Quaker garb has been drab, gray, and white. Although some of the following illustrations show the Quaker women taking care to avoid worldly gaudiness, others were quite colorful.

As with most other fashions, inspiration for the cut of Quaker dress often originated in Paris, considered the center of fashion and taste. But the

ILLUSTRATION 27.

grays, sage greens, and somber browns. In the social neighborhoods in Philadelphia, apparently the plain Friends were so accustomed to seeing brilliant dressing in others that they did not take alarm at these colors, despite all they had said and written on the subject of dress in the official character.[16]

In a day when fashionable ladies were wearing sack-back dresses of brocade over large oblong hoop petticoats and powdered hair piled high on the head, one New England Quaker lady in Salem, Massachusetts, in 1750, chose to modify her wedding dress, as shown in Illustration 27.

Made of white satin, the bodice fastened in the back with hooks and eyes; the upper part of each sleeve was embroidered with a rosebud in white silk. (The long, full sleeves were evidently of a later date; ruffles of sheer lawn like the fichu probably finished the shorter sleeves when the gown was first worn.) The reticule (a small handbag, which was introduced late in the century) was carried by hand and was of a white, lustrous, paper-thin silk called lutestring, embroidered (like the sleeves) in white silk. Her cap was in the shape so popular at that time among women of all classes. The hair was arranged very simply, drawn back softly over the ears and into a knot at the back.

Some Quaker dress styles used a fine white lace apron, whereas others had a colored apron. One bride in the middle of the eighteenth century wore a sprigged muslin gown. Illustrations 28 and 29 also present Quaker wedding dresses.

Illustration 28 shows a dress of brown ribbed silk, worn by a Quaker bride in 1766 in Mansfield, New Jersey. The costume included a white net cap, gray taffeta shawl, a white lawn kerchief, and a white "modesty piece" tucked inside the bodice. The bride also wore short gray silk mitts.

Illustration 29 shows a tan taffeta dress of 1798, which pointed out the latter part of the century's fondness for the overdress: open in front with full skirt plumped out over petticoats. It had three-quarter-length tight sleeves and a low neck with gather strings tying in front, filled in

expression of Quaker simplicity remained in the absence of superfluous adornments. Members were encouraged to avoid bright colors, but no rigid laws were passed forbidding them. Favorite colors most often used continued to be the soft

ILLUSTRATION 28.

ILLUSTRATION 29. *33013*

with a white lawn kerchief. The bonnet was tan quilted silk, with ribbon ties; beneath it was a white cap.

Among the formal and elegant fabrics coming from Europe at this time were figured damasks (in pinks, blues, or bright, clear yellows) and brocades in lovely colors. The figured silks had floral designs smaller than in previous years; some had wide stripes with floral sprays and embroideries in colored silks. White satin was also a favored fabric for gowns.

A Philadelphia woman wore the white satin dress in Illustration 30 at her marriage in 1760. It had a bodice cut low in front and finished with tabs below the waist. The elbow-length tight sleeves were finished with a graduated ruffle of lace. The gown was trimmed with lace in festooned flounces, or "falbalas," according the the prevalent fashion. The back view shows the deep pointed bodice to which the skirt was gathered with numerous small pleats.

Two early methods of communicating fash-

ILLUSTRATION 30.

ILLUSTRATION 31.

ion—from its source to the recipient—were the fashion doll and the fashion plate. The circulation of dolls clad in miniature replicas of full-scale garments originated at an early date; dolls were sent from France to many European countries. Fashion was previewed through these beautiful models, which imparted information about current styles and created a favorable climate for accepting them.

These circulating miniature beauties were dolls of wax, porcelain, china, bisque, or papier-

mâché, and tremendous excitement greeted them when they reached American shores. They were known as "fashion babies," and dolls for years were referred to as doll-babies.

It is interesting to note that, in 1759, George Washington ordered a dressed wax doll for his three-year-old stepdaughter, and in 1762 he purchased two fashion-dressed dolls, one costing a guinea ($5.25). Both of these orders were sent to London. [17]

Dolls with fashionable attire continued to be

ILLUSTRATION 32.

imported until the end of the nineteenth century. They were a constant source of inspiration for styles that brides could adopt. One of these fashionable beauties is shown in Illustration 32 in bridal attire (c. 1870). She wears an antique satin gown trimmed with lace and seed pearls. Her headpiece is of pearls and silk flowers; the veil is of embroidered lace. Her beautifully made undergarments are of fine cotton trimmed with tucks, lace, and insertion lace. Crocheted stockings and high white kid boots adorn her legs.

These fashion babies merit more than passing notice; they were small models, showing the very latest ideas in dress and were sent by Paris modistes (fashionable clothing dealers) to London and other large cities. Mademoiselle Martin, a well-known modiste of Marie Antoinette's time, sent fashionable doll models to the most distant parts of Europe.

The Quakers, too, used the quaint dolls and sent them to distant Friends to show what was worn in the cities. The models—one can hardly call them dolls, as they were no playthings—were made with great care. Much thought, time, and effort went into the construction of their clothes.

One of these models was in the exact dress of Rebecca Jones, a well-known Philadelphia Friend who lived from 1739 to 1818. This doll had a bonnet with a soft crown, and she wore a very large cape ending in three points.

Another fashion baby in Quaker dress was named Patty Rutter. Dressed in 1782 by Miss Sarah Rutter of Philadelphia, she was sent to Mrs. Samuel Adams of Quincy, Massachusetts. Her dress was drab silk, her bonnet and shawl white silk. At her side hung a chatelaine, with watch and pencil. The doll and her costume are still intact.[18]

Although these are records of Quaker dolls, the majority of the small fashion models wore fine silks, satins, and brocades in "fancy" and elaborate dresses—primarily in the French mode.

Artists, editors, designers, manufacturers, and merchants all wanted to promote interest in fashion. It is believed that *Le Cabinet des Modes* was the first publication completely devoted to supplying news about fashion. It was not a technical pattern book; it was published fortnightly (every two weeks) with plates colored by hand. Produced in Paris in 1785, it included both male and female costumes, hairdressing, interior decoration, and even included carriages—a primary status symbol.[19]

The woman with a taste for chic, fashionable clothes depended a great deal on fashion plates. The appealing dolls and colorful fashion plates did much to acquaint American women with styles from abroad and supply them with the news of trends that they wanted. Those with means had dresses made using heavy brocades and silks, and the look of fashion in this last half of the eighteenth century in the colonies was feminine and graceful.

One such graceful creation is a Watteau sack style, part of the wedding outfit of a young bride of Hope Lodge, White Marsh, Pennsylvania, who was married in 1752 (See Ill. 33). The gown was ivory taffeta, brocaded with clusters of flowers in pinks, yellows, and red-purples with green leaves. There was additional background brocading of sprays and small leaf motifs in stripes, all

ILLUSTRATION 33. *Brocaded ivory taffeta trousseau dress with Watteau back (1752).*

ILLUSTRATION 34.

ILLUSTRATION 35. *This handsome taupe silk brocade wedding dress was worn around 1776. It had a brocade overskirt and a quilted petticoat.*

ILLUSTRATION 36. *This 1783 wedding dress in pale green and white ribbed silk, with a small floral stripe in the brocade, is an Americanized Louis XVI style. The bodice is pointed front and back; the sleeves are elbow-length with lace ruffle. The skirt, open in front, is longer in back; it has an underskirt in the form of an apron.*

in self-color. It is believed to have been made in Spitalfields, England. The style was known as a robe *à la Française;* it had an open front, trimmed with graduated serpentine pleating with pinked edges, a Watteau back, and pinked falbalas on elbow-length sleeves. The bodice was lined with linen. The petticoat was pleated onto two bands

that tied at the sides. The lower edge of the front panel was trimmed with deep pinked ruffles set on in serpentine curves.

In January 1759, the wedding of the young Colonel George Washington and widow Martha Custis typified the height of gaity and elegance in colonial Virginia. The particulars of this wedding

ILLUSTRATIONS 38 & 39. *Ill. 38 is a faithful copy of the border motif that appeared down the open-front overskirt and at the train; also at the hem of the underskirt and the sleeves. Single, small floret clusters were painted elsewhere on the linen (Ill. 39). With this gown was a full-length wedding cape; it had a wide, pointed collar, front opening, and its hemline was outlined with a wide band of white ermine. The cape also had a taffeta lining.*

ILLUSTRATION 37.

ILLUSTRATION 40. *All the features of the emerging Empire style are evident in this alluring dress of the last year of the century. This is a fine example of the transition period: a wedding dress of soft, clinging satin and mull. The overdress had a high waistline and a surplice line; the back fullness was achieved by soft pleats caught to the high waistline, thus hanging free to form the train.*

ILLUSTRATION 41. *Front view of the gown in Ill. 40.*

ILLUSTRATION 43. *Detail of the silk fly-fringe on the overdress of the gown in Ill. 40.*

ILLUSTRATION 42. *Back view of the gown in Ill. 40. The elbow-length sleeves were trimmed with folds of georgette crepe, caught with circlets of artificial pearls. The underskirt was of white India mull, embroidered with fine metallic gold dots.*

ILLUSTRATION 44.

and a description of the bride's dress are recounted in Chapter 17.

The white silk brocade dress in Ill. 34 was worn by a Salem, Massachusetts, woman in about 1765. It is believed to be her wedding dress. The back had the graceful Watteau pleat; the handsome brocade was embroidered with silver tinsel and lace. The design was an open trailing floral stripe with conventionalized flowers, and the fabric came from an earlier period. The dress has been altered. One often finds alterations, as the beautiful and costly fabrics could easily be remade into dresses for a daughter or granddaughter.[20]

With the threat of imposed taxes from Britain, American opposition grew until the king's authority to make laws directly affecting the colonies was no longer acceptable. Events led to the War of Independence, and sea travel and trade became more hazardous than ever. This meant limited goods were available from abroad, including dry goods and fine fabrics. As a result, a bride-to-be had to make provisions far in advance for her bridal apparel. Yet despite hardships in acquiring yard goods and making gowns at that time, women still managed to make lovely dresses.

The Transition Period

The years from 1790 to 1800 are referred to as the "transition period." The American republic was led by Presidents Washington and Adams. Both their First Ladies had good taste in clothing and had been influenced by the fashions from Europe. But at this period, Americans who looked to Paris for fashion assessment found great confusion. In 1789, the French Revolution had ravaged the spirit and nationalism of France, and the rebellion against nobility plainly evidenced itself in various fashions, some quite bizarre. Court fashions were gone. Paniers had disappeared, as had high, upswept, powdered hair and rich, brocaded materials.

In 1795, one young lady in Norwich, Connecticut, spent many months handpainting a floral border design on very fine linen, which she later used for her wedding dress (see Ill. 37). She styled the dress to suit her own taste, so it had more of the features of the dresses of the 1780s than those of fifteen years later. The bodice, slightly fitted, had a gathered fichu effect at the neckline, sewn into the center front seam and at the shoulder. The underskirt was softly gathered. The overskirt, gathered at the waistline, fell loosely to the floor in a semicircular cut to form a long train. There were no hoops, paniers, or padding. Its beauty was in the exquisite floral border painted in watercolors—red, yellow, blue, green, and purple.

The charming painting of Nelly Custis in her wedding dress (see Ill. 44) is in the downstairs "baby-sitting" children's room in Woodlawn Plantation, Virginia. Nelly Custis was George Washington's foster daughter, Eleanor Parke Custis; she married Washington's nephew, Lawrence Lewis, at Mount Vernon on February 22, 1799, Washington's last birthday. This artist's rendering, entitled *Washington's Last Birthday,* is a purely imaginary scene, painted one hundred years after the wedding took place; though not quite historically accurate, it does reflect the costumes of the late 1700s.

As the eighteenth century closed, there were strong contrasts in cultures, particularly in the attire of the various ethnic groups in the United States. Puritan peoples still retained much of the reserve characteristic of them. Among the Germans who came to America were the Moravians, a simple, industrious people. Their love feasts, like those of the Dunkards, were joyous congregational participations. Firm rulings, however, were held by the Moravian community in provincial Pennsylvania. The Moravian group was divided into a number of choirs or bands. The bonnets worn by the sisters were usually made of white straw with plain ribbon, the color of which formed the distinction of each group (choir): white was worn by the widows, blue by the married women, rose by the unmarried, and red by girls from fourteen to eighteen years old.

There was a ruling against jewelry, lace, parasols, and fans, among other accessories. Although there was avoidance of all unnecessary adornment, there was no austerity. One bride's wedding dress (still extant) was of white satin, trimmed with gauze roses and ribbonwork. It had a short waist and little puffed sleeves and was worn in 1790. The woman who wore it also had a white gauze shawl with one long corner embroidered in an elaborate pattern; this she wore with a black velvet dress. She attended church in this dress, accompanied by a page carrying her train and a foot-stove.[21]

From a portrait we have the description of a particular dress worn by Countess Zinzendorf, who was the wife of the leader of the Moravians in America. She wore a close-fitting cap with ribbons of blue (the distinctive trimming for a Moravian matron) tied under the chin. The unmarried sisters usually dressed in white with a handkerchief pinned around their shoulders, a close-fitting cap with rose-pink ribbons, and their hair brushed back, out of sight.[22]

Dresses throughout the last half of the century retained long, flowing lines, detailed construction, and rich materials; they structurally followed the female figure outline with added drapery. The period can truly be called a graceful age.

Part II

Nineteenth Century

4

The Empire Style:
Classical Revival (1800-1820)

At the beginning of the nineteenth century, the seat of the U.S. government was transferred from Philadelphia to Washington. The charming Abigail Adams was the first "lady" of the White House. Americans were beginning to show their own sense of fashion, yet styles and materials continued to come from Europe, predominantly from London and Paris. And the fashions from France, after its turbulent revolution, were anything but conservative.

A young bride, eager to stay current with the latest mode, knew full well how limited materials were in the States. She would have to find the lines of the Empire style from journals, a few fashion magazines, or letters from abroad. She might have wished to be fairly demure in her adaptation of dress, or perhaps might have chosen the very height of the prevailing fashion.

Dresses during this period followed the image of classical Greek statuary with the silhouette like an architectural column. The general contour of a dress started with a high waistline and continued through a full-length straight skirt, usually of sheer, diaphanous material. Frequently the dress had a drawstring at the neck and below the breast, so that the dress could be pulled in and draped according to the wearer's wish.

Predictably, the standard neckline soon be-

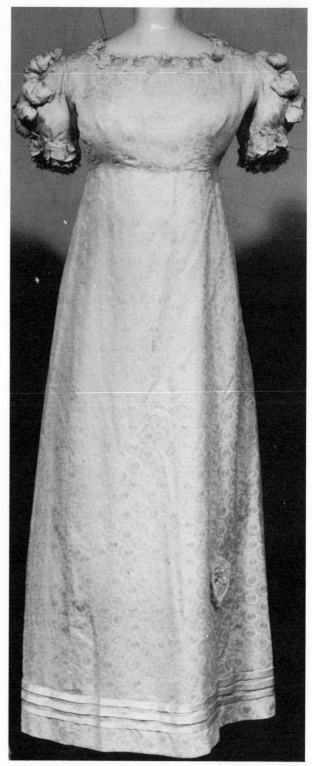

ILLUSTRATION 45.   ILLUSTRATION 46.

ILLUSTRATION 47. *Artist's rendering of an 1812 gown.*

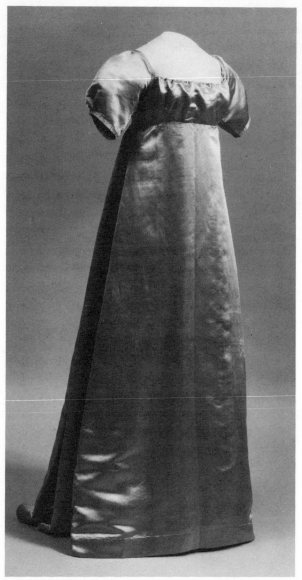

ILLUSTRATION 48.

ILLUSTRATION 49.

came lower and lower, the waistline higher and higher, the dress scantier and tighter, and the one thin petticoat often discarded. No corsets were worn in this period; the body's outline was clearly seen as gowns clung closely to the form. Some gowns included trains, and these, too, grew longer and longer.

The wedding gown in Illustration 45 possessed a style and fabric typical of the period (1800). Made of white satin brocade with a vertical stripe in a stylized floral design ending in a deep border brocaded pattern, the gown had an easy fullness but no train. A satin sash graced the high Empire waistline, with a large satin rosette, and the dress had short, puffed sleeves. Another dress (see Ill. 46) with no train was worn in 1804. Made of white silk damask in an all-over floral design, it had a square neck with lace and short sleeves. Satin bands and a lace rosette decorated the skirt.

The wedding dress in Illustration 47, from

ILLUSTRATION 50.

1812, was made of ivory figured moiré taffeta. Its wide, square neck was outlined with irridescent sequins and a scallop design in pearl beads. The Empire bodice had vertically stitched cording in front and was laced in back. Pearl beads finished the very short puffed sleeves. To keep the shape of the puff, a band of ribbon wire eight inches long supported the sleeves. True to the Empire mode, the skirt was straight in front, full and trained in back. The bottom was finished with loops of chiffon caught at intervals with two strands of pearl beads, and below that a fold of chiffon. Two pleated ruffles of chiffon edged with narrow taffeta box pleats finished the hem.

Another wedding dress (1820) of very simple lines was Quaker in origin. Made of pale yellow silk twill fabric, it had soft gathers above the high waistline and at the neckline and was gently shaped by four darts at the upper skirt. Long, tight sleeves had small, flared cuffs at the wrist. Cording of self-material was the only ornamentation at the neck, shoulder seam, and two rows above the hem.

When we look at the costumes of this or any period we can see that wherever in the world one happens to be, the influence of universal mode of dress is strong—and it is bound to be imitated.

Illustration 48 shows an 1809 Quaker wedding gown of gray satin that followed the fashion of the Empire period. Quakers' dresses were correspondingly shorter-waisted and low-necked, as were the other styles of the day.

The 1817 sheer taffeta wedding dress in Illustration 49 shows tasteful simplicity of line. No applied trimmings destroy the effective draping of the soft material. The back is gathered very full. Dresses like this—without folds and with plain, slim lines—were in fashion until the 1830s; they remained basically unchanged. Com-

ILLUSTRATION 51.

ILLUSTRATION 52.

pared to the elaborate costumes of the previous ages, these narrow, straight gowns of 1800 were very simple constructions. Gone was the tedious, time-consuming labor that went into the heavy woven and embroidered costumes of the Middle Ages, the Renaissance styles, the Elizabethan farthingales, or the French-inspired paniers. Yet complexity was to reign again in the not-too-distant future, in what would be known as the Victorian age.

Two interesting practices of the early 1800s helped achieve the full fashion look so desirable then. One was a little stuffed pad or bag sewn inside the high-waisted center back to prevent the skirt from falling into the hollow of the back. Another was the "Grecian bend"—a curious fashion of the years 1815–1819, when a forward stoop was considered the style. To heighten this effect a small bustle was worn high up under the skirt. We see this reappear in 1868.

Illustration 50 shows a youthful and attractive pale ivory silk twill wedding gown of 1812 with high Empire puffed sleeves above the lower sleeves of embroidered net. The pink bow at the neckline and pink slippers show the introduction of color on wedding apparel. The bride wore stockings of ivory knitted silk, embroidered from toe to midcalf with dots, and pink kid flat-soled shoes with white silk ribbon ties and trim.

Handmade lace, called heirloom lace today, has always been treasured by brides for fine wedding dresses. Prior to 1800, making lace by hand attained its highest art form. Until 1800, garment makers and personal dressmakers had relied almost entirely upon goods, trim, and accessories from Europe. Beginning in 1803, lace was made by machine and was called Patent lace. How happy was the bride who could now have a wedding dress of this delicate and once very expensive fabric! She would no longer have to wait while the lace was made—slowly, tediously—by hand.

About the same time a machine was invented that could make net. In Philadelphia, in 1815, the manufacture of silk trimmings was introduced; and in Baltimore, in 1829, silk ribbon was first manufactured. The availability of these items in the States was a great convenience; previously, a long wait was necessary for imported accessories. After 1819, when the *Savannah,* the first steamboat to cross the Atlantic, traveled from Savannah, Georgia, to Liverpool, England, fabrics and fashion news could be brought back to American shores in much shorter time.

Women longed to copy and own fashion chosen by women of nobility, fame, or prestige. As early as the beginning of the nineteenth century—with more distribution of wealth, increased facilities for travel and commerce, and the lowered cost of machine-made materials—all women could finally copy the dress of society women. Fashion news from France, for example, now began to reach Americans through magazines, journals, and books and by the dolls dressed in latest Parisian modes; the latter were sent with regularity to the many countries of Europe as well as to America. Manufacturers, too, strove to further their own commercial interests.

All these factors led to the desire for constant change, particularly on the part of a woman of wealth or position who wished to be exclusive in her wardrobe. She also became very secretive about the details of each gown, so that they could not be copied immediately.

Of singular interest in this respect is the description of a bridal dress of June 1816 from an English fashion plate (see Ill. 51). Made of striped French gauze over a white satin slip, the bottom of the frock was superbly trimmed with a deep flounce of Brussels lace, surmounted by a single tuck of bias white satin and a wreath of roses. Above the wreath were two tucks of the satin.

> We refer our readers to our print for the form of the body and sleeve; it is particularly novel and tasteful, but we are forbidden either to describe it, or to mention the materials of which it is composed. The one dress we have just described is a wedding dress which has recently been finished for a young lady of high distinction.[23]

Although the account would not specify who the bride was, almost everyone guessed that this wedding gown was designed for HRH Princess Charlotte of Wales. This was her marriage year.

The fashion plate in Illustration 51 shows the

hair low at the sides and parted so as to show the entire forehead. Such ornaments as an aigrette (a tuft of feathers worn on the head) with pearls in front, a sprig of French roses at the back of the head, earrings, necklace, and bracelets of pearl, white kid gloves, and white satin slippers complete the costume.

The Wearing of White

An often-asked question is, "When was white accepted as the correct or traditional color?" In *Two Centuries of Costume in America,* Alice Morse Earle writes that the earliest fashion plate found with a conventional white wedding dress appeared in 1818 (see Ill. 52). It had no wedding veil. Mrs. Earle relates that in November 1817 a woman who married a commodore wore white canton crêpe; this bride's pretty wardrobe was wholly of cottons: canton crêpe and India mulls, no silk among any of the dresses.

White satin and lace replaced the glittering brocades and silver muslins, according to another source. The bridal veil, practically nonexistent in the eighteenth century, also made a comeback in the trend toward classical fashions. Widows were forbidden the use of white, as were those known not to be virgins (in the latter case, white was often mixed with colors if a bride had not been married previously).[24]

Likewise, it was prescribed that flowers composing the wreath and bouquet would be white. Orange flowers were favored, but where they could not be procured, white rosebuds substituted. Lily of the valley was preferred to either.[25]

The rules regarding the use of white set a precedent and became a tradition. The symbol-ism suggested that white was an emblem of the innocence and purity of girlhood. But white was also a symbol of happiness and peace. This is not a recent concept; the early Romans always wore white on occasions of rejoicing—birth and feast days. The white rose was an emblem of joy among the Greeks, too. And the Patagonians painted the whole body white on the eve of the wedding ceremony.[26]

In America the tradition of wearing white for weddings began about 1800. One of the main contributing factors is that heavy silks and brocades were not in vogue. They did not provide the soft drapery needed to attain a clinging effect that thinner fabrics did. The fabrics most used for evening wear and weddings were muslin, mull, lawn, batiste, organdy, thin silks, gauzes, light voiles, linens, and cashmeres. These were primarily available in white. East Indian merchants were kept very busy supplying the thin white materials to satisfy the fashion market.

An interesting shopping list of wedding items is found in a tiny satin-covered book from Kingston, Rhode Island. The 1802 book lists many fabrics, including dimity, organdy, lawn, and linen. No silk is mentioned. There is also mention of "money sent to Antwerp." This was probably for the purchase of Flemish lace, which was fashionable at the time. The list reads:

Necklace and Case.	$ 52.
8 yds. Muslin 14/per yard.	20.
5½ yds. lace 5 dolls. per yd.	27.
5¾ yds Dimity @ 5/per yard	4.9
1 doz. Stockings @ 9/	18.
4 yds. of Calico @ 5/6	4.
Dressing Case and Comb.	3.
Piece of Linen	25.
3 yds of Cambric.	7.

Piece of Cambric	22.
6 yds of Muslin	20.
4 yds of figured Cambric	5.1
5 prs Stockings at 8/	5.1
4 yds of Dimity	9.4
9 yds of Cambric	2.4
Money sent to Antwerp	150.
Ditto for furniture making	150.
Money carried to Boston	110.
26 yds of Diaper at 3/6	15.
5 yds of Ditto @ 2/	2.
Tea set of China	15.
Dinner set ditto	69.
Tea trays	7.
Bill of Geoffroy	100.

The bride for whom these items were imported, Madam Randolph, was married July 4, 1802, at Newport. Her husband was a young Virginia planter who came north with his own carriage and horses. After the wedding they returned to the plantation on the James River.[27]

The Empire style was a unique look most easily recognized by its high waistline and simplicity of line. In dressmaking, there is as much challenge in creating a good-looking plain garment as there is an elaborate one. In the twenty years from 1800 to 1820, the challenge was met; some lovely dresses remain as testament to that fact.

5

The Coquette and the Demure Bride: The Picturesque and Romantic Look (1820-1850)

Fashions in the late twentieth century change so rapidly that we can easily recognize "last year's fashion" and "this year's new look." It seems amazing to us that the simple Empire style lasted for the greater part of twenty years. During the many years that the Empire style was in vogue, there was little that fashion could do to further simplify the line; so decorative ornament was added. Increasingly, garments were festooned and trimmed with braid, ribbons, and innumerable dressings. This trend ushered in an age of fussiness that today we consider overdone. Excessive ornamentation was the style not only in clothing, but also in architecture, furniture, and the arts. As the nineteenth century progressed, this ostentatiousness increased, distorting the form of the female body.

When the statuesque look of 1800–1820 disappeared, garment outlines were no longer slim and vertical, but instead became wide above and below the waistline. Again, the corset was worn, and it defined the waistline, making it appear very small. Lacing became progressively tighter and more severe. The angular outline that had been developing for some time reached its height in the 1830s. Flared shoulders and hem formed two triangles; the apexes met at the waist, forming an X.

The 1822 wedding dress in Illustrations 53 and 54 is noteworthy because of two particular features: the beauty of the cool brown color of the medium-weight satin and the exquisitely fine hand-stitching. The style of the dress shows the demigigot sleeve, very full to below the elbow,

ILLUSTRATION 53. *Typical of dress construction in the 1820s is this brown satin wedding dress (1822). From the tiny waist, the skirt falls to the floor, with 111 inches around the hem. There are two placket openings in the side front of the skirt, and inside the waistline seam is sewn a tiny pocket.*

ILLUSTRATION 54. *Back view of the dress in Ill. 53.*

tapering to a very tight sleeve at the wrist.

The outward appearance of dress comes from the structure of the underclothing. The corset of these early years was no mere piece of fabric. It had the form of a long, fitted underbodice shaped to the body by the insertion of small triangular pieces of reinforcing material called gussets, which gave roundness to the breasts. Gussets at the bottom allowed for rounded hips. The corset had a center front busk (a strip of steel,

whalebone, or other stiffening material placed in the front of a corset) and bones for lacing the center back. Later, more seams were added and more bones, sometimes with a basque for the hips instead of gussets. This was the basic cut and design of corsets during most of the nineteenth century, until the late 1880s.[28]

Writers on historical costume tell of young women who were more than willing to suffer the pain of tight lacings for the admiration of their

ILLUSTRATION 55. *This charming white satin wedding gown was worn in 1824 by a Petersburg, Virginia, bride. Made with a deep trimming of white gauze, it was held in place by bows of gauze bound with white satin.*

ILLUSTRATION 56.

audience, whether close relatives or people in society. Everything worn was constricting: tight stays (corsets), tight shoes, tight garters, tight waistbands, armholes, and bodices. Even men were influenced by the drawn-in look; many wore corsets and tightly tailored clothing.

Since plumpness was fashionable, sometimes a pad stuffed with wool, bustle fashion, was worn under skirts to increase the rounded look. Dresses, shortened to ankle length, were heavily trimmed and generally very décolleté for evening. Bodices remained lined.

One common style was the crossing over of material in the front of the bodice in pleated folds or trim (see Ill. 56). This creamy white crêpe gown (1825) has large sleeves puffed at the top,

ILLUSTRATION 57.

tight from elbow to wrist; there are net over-sleeves. The gown has satin piping trim. (For another gown with diagonal folds across the front, see Ill. 73.)

When a wedding dress had no train, it was called a "frock." When trained, it was called a "gown." Yet there were few, if any, gowns with trains in this period. A particularly lovely English fashion plate depicting a wedding dress appeared in January 1827. In the description of this dress the word *corsage,* meaning a tight-fitting sleeveless bodice or jacket resembling a corset, was used. This term, which originated in the Middle Ages toward the end of the thirteenth century, appeared repeatedly in early costume descriptions. The gown in Illustration 57 was a frock of sprigged lace of a very fine Brussels pattern. The corsage was circular, plain in front, full in back, with a low neckline of a double row of the same lace, flounced.

The sleeves were very full, regulated by seven or eight drawstrings from the shoulder to below the elbow, then plain to the wrist. Scallops

hemmed the edge of the dress below a deep flounce. A broad white satin sash with bows on the right side finished the waistline. A white satin slip with a wadded hem at the bottom was worn under the lace gown.

Hair styles in this period were very elaborate. In this same print (Ill. 57), the hair is parted in front with three large curls on the left side. Above are bows of white satin and crêpe lisse, a smooth, fine gauze silk often used for ruffles and trimmings. On the right side are sprigs of myrtle and two full-blown white roses.

To complete the entire wedding costume were three rows of pearls, clasped in front by a brilliant gem; long pearl earrings; a cameo bracelet of pearls and emeralds; white kid gloves and white satin slippers.

One highly descriptive account of a midwinter 1829 New England wedding can be found in a letter written by Emily G. Swift (Mrs. E. G. Swift) to her brother in New Haven. It was penned in the usual delicate handwriting using the quill pen and employing the long, flowing "S" letter. From the description, one has the feeling of place, of seeing the actual garments, and of the festivities surrounding the nuptials. Evidently, a heavy snowfall had melted on the roads, and a sleigh could not be used, necessitating the change to a wagon or carriage instead. This letter is presented in its original form.

Friday, Feb. 13th, 1829

Dear Brother,
Sabbath evening Henry and his brother came to America and brought Nancy with them. On Monday we prepared for wedding. Henry and Robert were obliged to procure a wagon the sleighing having

wasted on Sunday so much that a sleigh
would not run. On Tuesday about seven
o'clock in the evening about thirty five
weddingers were collected and a short ceremony by Mr Bronson united Robert and
Mary Ann in the bond of matrimony. Henry
and Nancy first entered the room followed
by R. and M. The groom and groomsman
were dressed in blue white vests trimmed
with pale blue cord white gloves silk stock-
ing morroco shoes. The bride and bridesmaid were dressed alike in muslin skirts
trimmed with a deep flounce on the bottom,
white satin spencers with long sleeves lace
on the wrists and necks white shoes, points
on the neck of spencers white satin ribbons
on their neck—pins rings and chains. Heads
dressed with combs puffs curls three white
feathers each and a white rose. I never saw
persons look better in my life.

A tea two kinds of wine and brandy in the
evening. The second day Wednesday after
breakfast the company rode until dinner.
Dined at Mary's father's. The dinner table
was filled with turkeys chickens oysters coffee tea . . . of all kinds pies, etc. etc.
Wednesday I had a party, of about thirty to
Tea. Cake dressed with frosting and tasty
preserves and other good things for a tea-
table. Cake in the middle of the table in the
form of a pyramid three other kinds about
the table arranged with all the taste I possess. Tea and coffee. After tea the Maluga
and brandy went freely around after which
almonds filberts beachnuts walnuts and ap-
ples were served. Our west room after Tea
was filled with chairs along the sides the
ladies seated dancing commenced with

ILLUSTRATION 58.

music. Violins and two flutes. This lasted
until twelve in the evening. There were ten
took breakfast and dinner with me and
dancing and whist was not wholly forsaken
on Thursday. Thursday evening Henry and
Nancy in front of the carriage, Robert and
Mary Ann behind. Walter and Amy Swift in

ILLUSTRATION 59. *Marie Caroline, Duchess of Berry, France (c. 1835).*

ILLUSTRATION 60. *Queen Amalia, Germany (1835).*

ILLUSTRATION 61. *Mademoiselle Henrietta Sontag, German singer and actress (1830).*

a gig. Moses Swift and Lady Thomas and myself went to Dover were cordially received by all. The company were seated and after the girls dressed Henry and Robert waited on the ladies in the room changing partners—after they entered Henry introduced the bride to her new parents. I must not forget to mention that Captain Reston was among the guests. Thursday at our house while some of the party were at dinner the Captain in a very graceful manner began dancing about the table and singing, "Molly put the kettle on" when he caught the bottom of his pantaloons on the top of the andiron—pulled it over on to a teapot broke the top of it fell his whole length and tore his pantaloons badly. Be assured that we have had a good wedding nothing but your company to have made the times complete. . . . Mary Ann is at father's now will stay until Saturday or Sunday I have almost worn out myself. I have done for them what I would not do for myself. . . ."[29]

The spencer jacket described in this wedding was a very short jacket, named for Lord Spencer, which usually had a puff or turnover collar and was lined with fur or swansdown when worn in winter (see Ill. 58). Fashion bulletins from 1800 to 1830 almost always included the spencer.

The young American woman was rural. In the 1820s and 1830s, eleven-twelfths of the population lived outside the larger cities and towns, showing a strong percentage of agricultural over manufacturing and commercial interests. The young United States was growing very rapidly in extent and area—in the spread of civilization rather than in an increase of population density. The 1840 census showed that since 1830 the average population of the country had not increased by so much as one person to the square mile.[30]

This was the time of internal wars and treaties, of American Indians retreating to the West, their spirit broken; years when the slave trade was flourishing and new states were being admitted into the Union. These were the times, too, of buccaneers and piracy against shipping; in 1822, more than twenty pirate ships were captured among the islands in the West Indies. Disasters also made their mark on the robust new nation. In 1835, the fire in the lower part of New York City laid to ashes thirty acres of buildings, 529 houses and pieces of property. Museum staffs to-

ILLUSTRATION 62.

day remind us that much knowledge of costume and fabrics (as well as the actual clothing of long ago, including wedding dresses) has been lost because of devastating fires in the cities.

But for a growing America, this period was free for a time from revolution both at home and

ILLUSTRATION 63.

still originated in France, England, Germany, and Italy. News reached America three or more weeks after a social event in Europe had taken place. The American woman most likely had access to one or more European publications. She looked at all that came from abroad and then modified and adapted the whims of current fashion to her own satisfaction.

The American woman's wardrobe would be influenced by what she would see of such women as the French Duchess of Berry, Marie Caroline, (see Ill. 59), a colorful personality who lived during the bitter insurrections in France in the 1830s.

Perhaps the young bride-to-be was influenced by the high style of the German Princess Amalia, of the House of Oldenburg, who married Otho of Bavaria in 1835 and became Queen Amalia (see Ill. 60). Their reigning court was established in Athens, Greece.

German simplification of the post-Empire style (1820–1840) was known as the Biedermeier style. Then there was the high style of the German singer and actress Henrietta Sontag (see Ill. 61), who had earned worldwide regard for her beautiful voice and dramatic skills in opera and on stage. Born on the Rhine in Coblenz and educated in Prague, Sontag became the pride of Berlin. At the height of her career, she married Count Rossi, an Italian nobleman, the ambassador of Sardinia to The Hague. Like Jenny Lind, she made appearances in America and was just as famous and successful a personality.

Illustration 62 shows an ivory figured satin wedding gown of 1834. The fitted bodice was pointed at center front, with a back hook-and-eye closing. It had a straight, off-the-shoulder neckline, pleated bands, and a bow in front. The very full sleeves, tapering to narrow wrists, were stiffened with a linen lining. The shoes that were

abroad; and for the infant republic, the founders' original scheme of government was successful. President Monroe's second term of office coincided with a period known as the "era of good feeling." This mood had some bearing on the design of dresses made in the United States. So, too, did the restrictions of geographical locations, the limitations of transport and trade, and the availability of fabrics, trimmings, and accessories.

Adaptation was the key word for the American woman who was taking fabric and needle in hand to design her most important raiment: her wedding clothes. She was, for the most part, out of the mainstream of a fashion-conscious society—unlike her European sisters, who were either involved in court circles or could look to influences from fashionable women. Until the 1830s, there was no American fashion leader. Clothing styles

ILLUSTRATION 64. *This wedding dress (c. 1837) of gold silk damask is figured with a small crown-and-rose motif. There are six horizontal folds at the yoke and two sections of small longitudinal pleats from upper sleeve to elbow.*

ILLUSTRATION 64.

worn with this dress were heeless and square-toed. The label inside them reads: "S. HALE, LADIES SHOE MAKER N.W. CORNER OF FOURTH & WALNUT, PHILADELPHIA."

Sleeves in this picturesque period took fascinating forms and diverse names:

Gabrielle sleeve (1820): full from shoulder to elbow, then fairly full to middle of forearm, ending in a deep cuff with lace band.

Marie sleeve (1825): full sleeve tied at intervals and at the wrist, forming puffs.

Gigot sleeve (1825): very full to below the elbow, then tighter to the wrist.

Demi-gigot: full at top, tight from elbow to wrist.

Mameluke (1827): full nearly to wrist.

Imbecile (1827): very full with longitudinal folds extending downward from elbow.

Donna Maria (1827): full and puffed to below elbow, then tighter to the wrists.

Beret sleeve (1829): sleeve formed from a very wide circle of fabric, resembling a beret headdress.

Leg-of-mutton sleeve (1830): very wide at shoulder, tapering down to wrist (worn by men and women in the Middle Ages, c. end of the fifteenth century).

Amadis (1830–31): tight, short cuff at wrist.

Du Barry (1830–31): puff above and below the elbow.

Montespan (1830–31): upper part full, band at elbow, and ruffle extending over part of the forearm.

Balloon-shaped (1832): large, inflated, and lined.[31]

Crinoline and down-filled tie-in pads were used to support large sleeve parts. By 1838, the sleeve again was round and tighter.

In the *Costumes de Modes* (a fashion publication) that came from Paris in October 1832, a wedding dress was shown that had the "picturesque" look (see Ill. 63). Women then coveted the wasp-waisted style, wearing sashes and ribbons or shaped, stiffened fabric to define the waistline. The picturesque look included enormously puffed sleeves, wide décolleté neckline, wasp-waist, full skirt, and trimmed poke bonnets. The dress in Illustration 63 used a great deal of lace, as did the

ILLUSTRATION 65.

ILLUSTRATION 66.

of picturesque and romantic-looking dresses, the hemline rose above the instep, sometimes above the ankle. It was the only period of the century in which this was true.

Only on rare occasions does one find a skirt and blouse worn for a wedding costume. In Illustration 65, the blouse was white pin-tucked batiste in a shirtwaist style. It had long balloon sleeves and a wristband of eyelet embroidery. There were tiny self-covered buttons at the waist front opening.

The light olive-green silk skirt was gored* and trimmed with blue buttons and blue ribbon in a zigzag pattern. A velvet sash was worn with it. It was not rare for a wedding costume to have two separate bodices, or blouses. One might be much dressier than the other. Since so many dresses in 1830 had low décolleté necklines, in this instance (see Ill. 65) the bride was either very modest, or the high-neck trim of the blouse was added later. This blouse and skirt was worn in the early 1830s.

Illustrations 67 through 72 show an ivory satin dress complete with all the accessories. Illustration 68 shows the dress alone, with its delicate edging detail down the front opening of the skirt. The bodice has eleven boned seams and twelve hooks and eyes at the center front closing, giving definite shape to the waist and bust. The inside of the bodice is furnished with four tie-strings at center front closing. There are three and a half yards at lower skirt edge. In Illustration 69 you can see the separate satin underskirt, which is more like an apron than a full, rounded petticoat; ten pleats face the center front. The separate lace bertha collar (see Ill. 70) has a delicate crocheted edge, ruching, and five rows of gathers decorated

*A panel or triangular piece of material inserted in a skirt to taper it or give it greater width or the desired shape.

veil. A wide satin sash defined the tiny waist. The arrangement of headdress was novel; the veil was interwoven with the smooth curls and thick braids of hair, lace, ribbons, pearls, and roses—all piled high on the head. The clusters of curls over the ears may have been false.

The waistline in the 1820s was round, following the body's natural contour. Around 1831, the waistline began to be sharply angled, gradually deepening into a deep point at the waist, similar to eighteenth-century styles. During these years

ILLUSTRATION 67.

ILLUSTRATION 70.

ILLUSTRATION 71.

ILLUSTRATION 68.

ILLUSTRATION 69.

ILLUSTRATION 72.

ILLUSTRATION 73. *This plum-colored silk wedding dress (c. 1835) is of New England origin. Mrs. John Adams had a similar gown, of soft, plum-colored Chinese crêpe, embroidered in silk from knee to hem.*

ILLUSTRATION 74. *White silk dress in woven floral pattern (1835).*

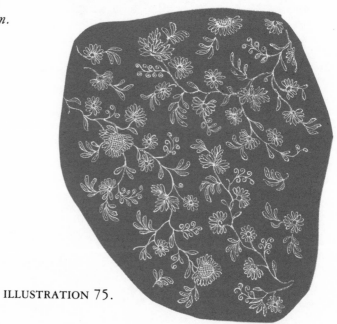

ILLUSTRATION 75.

ILLUSTRATION 76. *A gold silk dress with appliqué trim at neckline and waistline (1837).*

with small satin bows and lace edging. Illustration 71 is a detail of the separate lace sleeves. The cascade wreath (see Ill. 72) has a fragile appearance. It contains six organdy fabric flowers decoratively combined with cascades of lily-of-the-valley, orange blossoms and buds, and small flowers. To this wreath is attached the long, full veil of tulle with one gold satin line embroidered the length of the veil, one and a half inches from the edging.

The arrangement of hair was highly contrived during this period, sometimes giving an absurd appearance. It was often arranged into bunches of curls and ringlets at the temples, brushed smoothly up the back of the head, and twisted into loops and knots. This creation was held up by pins and combs, then enhanced with flowers, feathers, pearls, and ribbons.

For footwear, thin slippers with crossed ribbons at the instep and no heels were the style.

Huge sleeves disappeared after 1836. When a bride wore a short-sleeved dress, she wore with it long kid gloves with many buttons.

If recorded history of this newly emerged country leans heavily on male accomplishments and attitudes, something quite different was captivat-

ILLUSTRATION 77.

ILLUSTRATION 78.

ing the female mind. Women would play the part of lovely porcelain dolls as an escape from the harshness of reality. As women tried to emulate the beautiful, the romantic, the quaint, and even the fanciful, clothing fashioners went to extremes in creating this demure and fragile look. All things feminine—delicacy, smallness, frailty, beauty—were sought after, and fashion was the

vehicle for achievement. A dainty shoe, a tiny waist, soft, white hands, a transparent complexion, and the illusion of a frail body—no sacrifice was too great to achieve this effect.

The fabrics themselves lent much to the appearance of being fragile. A Monroe County, Georgia, girl wore a simple, white sheer bridal dress (summer 1837) delicately embroidered in a

ILLUSTRATIONS 79 & 80. *This gown was worn by a Bangor, Maine, bride in July 1838. The hairstyle was the fashion of the day.*

conventional floral pattern (see Ill. 75). Yellow and gold were still favorites for wedding dresses in the 1830s.

The pelerine, a short, shaped cape covering the shoulders, was an attractive, much-needed accessory to low-necked gowns. Illustrations 77 to 80 show to good effect a pale gold, fancy-weave silk damask gown with matching pelerine. The dress

had a fitted pointed bodice, with seams reinforced by stays. Decorated with interlaced bands at the top, the sleeves were full from elbow to wrist, gathered into a rounded cuff trimmed with three rows of self-binding. The full skirt had one-inch-wide pleats ending in an inverted pleat in front.

Illustration 81 shows the wedding dress of the young Frances Shippen, who was a member of

ILLUSTRATION 81.

ILLUSTRATION 82. *This dress is made of beautiful fabric, white challis with silk cross-barred design. The bodice has nine hooks and eyes in the back and is lined with white cotton cloth. Each cuff has three hooks and eyes. The full skirt is pleated to the bodice. Side seams of the bodice are finished with very fine satin piping.*

one of Philadelphia's earliest families. Five generations earlier, in 1668, Edward Shippen had come from England and settled in the colonies. The Shippen grandfathers were scientists and physicians, one a chief justice of the Supreme Court of Pennsylvania. The beauty of the dress was its simplicity; rows of ruching of dotted net around the neck and bows of ribbon were the only ornamentation. Accessories no doubt completed the picture. Although this was an 1838 wedding, the dress is primarily an eighteenth-century style, most likely the bride's choice. Two pairs of shoes and a kerchief accompany it.

Certainly, many delectable details of the mode of the day came from the fashion-loving Victoria Regina of England, who became queen at seven-

ILLUSTRATION 83. *Here is an artist's conception of a bride and groom before a clergyman (1847). The steel engraving is entitled "The Marriage."*

teen, in June 1837, and married in 1840.

As the calendar turned to the new decade of the 1840s, women found themselves in a subjugated, almost captive position socially. And the situation did not improve in the decades that immediately followed. Much of this image was brought on by women themselves, who had adopted an unrealistic concept of how they should live and dress. This concept came in part from the diminutive stature of Queen Victoria. In deference to her, the semblance of smallness was much sought after.

Leaning on fantasy was a favorite pastime for the young woman of the forties, especially the bride-to-be. A dreamer, and quite often impractical, she tried to create a bridal dress that would make her look like a fairy princess. To achieve this effect required a special structure as well as sheer and filmy materials. Many dresses were made of silk net, tulle, organdy, and gauze. Underneath the skirt was another whole domain of fabrics in several layers, which gave a bouffant, airy appearance.

At the same time women were indulging in fantasy, the times saw a resurgence in Christian practices and strivings for spiritual perfection. Philosophers and writers added to the ideal of the "inner light." Puritanism still existed to some degree; combined with a certain prudery, this resulted in a good amount of suppression and an emphasis on purity. Such a puritanical outlook affected the female population in particular. Brides did not have the openness, frankness, and lack of inhibition about relations between the sexes that we have today. Daily Bible readings and matters of morals were crucial to the man and woman of the 1840s, and they tried to live up to the rules they imposed on themselves. The bride of the 1840s came to her wedding ceremony with a pure state and a highly disciplined life-style.

Cultures are not one-dimensional, however. Along with religious fervor came coquettish behavior. According to Victor Hugo, God made coquettes once he was finished creating fools. But Benjamin D'Israeli (the British statesman and novelist) countered with a different view. He declared that the coquette pursued a career that required great abilities, infinite plans, and a light and airy spirit. He conceded that it was the coquette who provided all the amusements: suggested the riding parties, planned the picnics, and acted out the charades. In his poetic way he saw her as the stirring element amid the "heavy congeries of social atoms," the soul of the house, the salt of the banquet.

The young woman of 1840 could be oh so

ILLUSTRATION 84. *This 1846 fashion plate presents the then-ideal look of fashion and the female form.*

ILLUSTRATION 86. *This wedding dress (1844) used many yards of tan, green, gold, and beige leaf-figured satin. The long, full skirt was attached to the bodice with tiny accordion pleats. It had a center-back hook-and-eye closure. The bodice was lined in brown cotton twill.*

ILLUSTRATION 85. *This wedding dress of net was worn by a young New York City woman who was married in 1844.*

feminine and demure, or saucy and coquettish; but whichever was her aspiration, she longed for that frail, pale, almost helpless look and went to great pains to achieve it. To contrast men as strongly as possible was women's one exercise of power in a man's world.

America was still a rugged land, demanding rigorous strength to carve out cities and towns from the wilderness. Frail as a woman might appear, after her marriage she managed to do an unbelievable amount of heavy work as a mother and homemaker.

The fashion magazines now carried many beautiful fine-line steel engravings of the fragile-looking gowns of this decade. Wedding dresses were included among them.

The huge hat again came into vogue after 1839, reviving the eighteenth-century style. Its proportions and lines made it an artistic creation, becoming to almost everyone. When the hat was made of straw, a lining of gauze kept hair from becoming disarranged. At times, ribbons, flowers, or veils decorated it.

In this period, veils were still in general use, having been worn from about 1800 on. Sometimes they ornamented a bonnet. One could be inspired to fashion the veil in many ways: hanging from the crown of the bonnet, drawn over the face, or tied under the chin (see Ill. 91). It was the perfect device for a real coquette.

A shift of interest from decorative sleeves to full, bouffant skirts meant wearing more and more petticoats. Illustration 88 shows an 1843 morning wedding dress of cream-colored net with a girdle of silk cord. The skirt was ankle-length, full, and domed, finished with a deep double hem below a deep pleat. The bodice was fitted over a cambric foundation that had eight stays in the lining. Fullness was gathered into the shoulder

ILLUSTRATION 87. *No feature could have better given the impression of a small waist than that shown at center front of the dress pictured in this painting by German artist Stieler.*

seams with the net falling in loose folds, gathered into the pointed waistline in several rows of tightly gathered shirring. Tiny cream-colored cording trimmed the V-shaped neckline, the armholes, and shoulder seams. The three-quarter-length sleeves were tiered in eight equally spaced folds. A silk cord with tasseled ends passed through a loop. The style is very typical of the cut of dresses in the 1830s and early 1840s. Satin slippers cut square across the instep, with narrow

ILLUSTRATION 88.

ILLUSTRATION 89. *This gown (c. 1845) is similar
in cut to others of the period. Its distinctive feature is
the application of short, dangling silk balls on the
sleeves.*

ILLUSTRATION 90.

ILLUSTRATION 91.

ties and square toes and lined with linen, are preserved with seven-button-length kid gloves, laced with matching satin ribbon, tied in a bow at the sides of the cuff.

From one of the modish figures in the French court, the popular Princess Adelaide, came fashion influences in the 1840s (see Ill. 90). The sister of King Louis Philippe, Duke of Orleans, who represented the younger branch of the Bourbon dynasty, Adelaide exercised a benign influence on the court, extending a culture and style abroad.

When a bride wore a bonnet with her wedding dress, the veil could easily be fashioned on the bonnet in back of the brim. She may well have also carried a fringed, plaid shawl. All things Scottish were fashionable at this time, the influence coming from the British Isles. Queen Victoria's visits to Scotland in the 1850s only increased the great demand for plaids.

ILLUSTRATION 92. *An 1847 wedding dress.*

ILLUSTRATIONS 93 & 94. *An 1849 satin wedding dress and detail.*

ILLUSTRATION 95. *The charm of this 1849 dress is the airy feeling of sheer organdy, trimmed with matching satin ribbon. The bodice is shirred into a blunt point at the waistline, with short, horizontally tucked sleeves. The bodice is softly padded across the center-front bustline. The skirt is finished with three deep, horizontal tucks above the hem, above much of which is satin ribbon.*

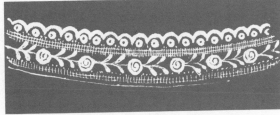

ILLUSTRATION 96. *The neckline detail of dress in Ill. 95.*

The women of still-rugged America had to cope with both reality and fantasy, and they foolishly strove for delicacy. It was the fashion seeker who most wanted this image of frailty. This self-inflicted style gave the young woman a tendency toward being dependent on the male, even to the extent of needing him nearby in case she suddenly fainted. Swooning was considered almost an accomplishment, particularly in suitable theatrical circumstances. A wedding provided an ideal setting for the wilting of a tiny, delicate form.

Yet these young women of fantasy also found themselves facing a difficult and often harsh life. In these years, the States were lining up on the

ILLUSTRATION 97. *A fashion plate depicting a bride and her dress (1847).*

ILLUSTRATION 98. *This white silk taffeta dress with fitted, boned bodice cut "en corset" was worn in 1849. It has very short scalloped sleeves in three tiers.*

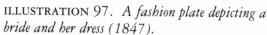

side of slavery or nonslavery; boundaries were being set after border skirmishes. Despite the fact that a bride looked like a breakable china doll, she often had a ruggedness that made her a good partner, one who would follow her husband to remote frontiers. At the end of this decade came the dramatic discovery of gold in California, and many city-reared young women took off their soft white wedding dresses and became true pioneers in the great West.

Illustrations 95 and 98 show two dresses of the year 1849. Enhanced by accessories, these gowns would flatter any bride.

In this chapter we have seen some examples of bridal dresses designed, made, and worn in the period that extended to the mid-nineteenth century. We have looked at the demure bride and the coquette. The age itself produced the coquette; in fact, it may have needed her, for there was much seriousness and strong discipline of manners. Young ladies were lectured by parents, schoolteachers, clergymen, writers, and poets. Despite all the restrictions on them, theirs was a picturesque and romantic time.

6

The Pioneer Bride

A pioneer is someone who first enters or settles a region, or who is first in any field of inquiry, enterprise, or progress. The pioneer bride, then, might be the first woman to be married in the New World, the first to flaunt a wide hoop skirt, or the first bride to wear a miniskirt or hot pants. Everything hinges on entering an unexplored area first.

No one was more qualified to be called a pioneer bride than the daughter of Puritans. After braving the perils of months on a sailing vessel, she stepped ashore on a primitive and unfriendly land where a hostile environment, harsh weather conditions, and vast, lonely miles greeted her.

We will, in this chapter, survey only the years from 1830 to 1885, which witnessed a great panorama of people in motion—the time when hoards of Americans were pressing toward the West. The pioneer legend seems so familiar that we think of the movement to the West as a time of gay excitement, a back-packing excursion. Yet the prospect of launching out into unknown territory was frightening, certainly not reasonable inducement for wedding plans. In fact, prospects were dim for any celebration. Who would there be to perform the marriage? Who might be the wedding guests? Most pioneer brides were married in their family's homestead in the East before starting on the journey west.

But those wedding dresses were never left behind! Tales of how a treasured dress was later used are many and varied. The gowns were packed in special boxes or small trunks and stored in a care-

ILLUSTRATION 99.

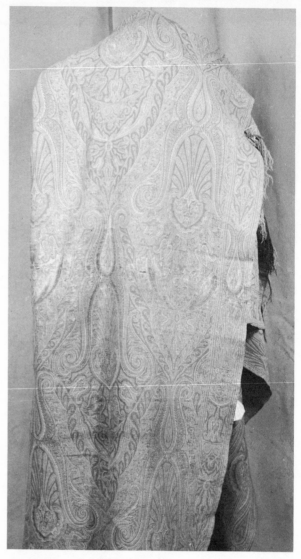

ILLUSTRATION 100.

fully chosen place in the covered wagon or oxcart. A gown gave the bride an unfading memory of home—verifiable proof that a real, substantial way of life existed "back East."

The women who pressed on to the West with their husbands had not lost, but only voluntarily and temporarily surrendered, a life more gracious and abundant than the one they would start. They carried with them a pattern of eighteenth-century elegance. They had known a social life steeped in traditions of distinction and separateness of social caste. Now, after 1776, traditions such as these were no longer tolerated.[32]

The earliest pioneer bride in the West did not know what it meant to spend months planning and fashioning her wedding trousseau. She could never indulge in hours of daydreaming and those leisurely pursuits surrounding a wedding. She never knew the luxuries of fashionable clothes or the niceties with which eastern girls were pampered. What she did know was that she was preparing to face the uncertainties of existence alongside her brave, strong trailblazer, and to share much of the toil in building a home in the new wilderness.

Such were the circumstances of the young Mar-

garet Beeman, who married John Neely Bryan,
lawyer, woodsman, pioneer, and founder of Dallas. They were wed on February 26, 1843, at Fort
Bonham, in the republic of Texas, in a simple
civil service. The groom wore a buckskin suit,
the bride a calico dress, and each wore moccasins.
After the wedding at the fort, they rode ponies to
Peter's Colony on the Trinity River (which later
became Dallas) and started life in a log cabin
there. The small cabin had been built by John
two years earlier.

This young pioneer had traveled west from his
Nashville home, contracting cholera on the Mis-
sissippi in 1833. Living with the Indians after his
recovery, he became restless to push on to the
great southern plains. He was the image of the
pioneer: always seen in flannel shirt, buckskin
coat and trousers, broad-brimmed hat, and moccasins on his feet; on the pommel of his saddle
was his rifle, pistol in holster and Bowie knife in
the scabbard.[33]

Another pioneer story concerns Sarah Bremley
Read, who married in England and traveled
across the plains—with her wedding dress—to
Utah. Her husband died on the trip, but she
continued on, arriving alone with her son. Her
wedding dress was her cherished keepsake. It was
of heavy white satin, had a tight bodice and a
full, ruffled, pleated skirt that reached to her ank-
les. The skirt had paniers on the sides. With it,
Sarah brought a blue hat with white feathers.[34]

An object of great beauty, and more treasured
by the pioneer bride than her wedding dress, was
her Paisley shawl. This article of clothing was
coveted by every woman, young or old, for
though a wedding dress was usually plain and
unadorned, the shawl was colorful and decorative. Most shawls were imported. They were ample and usually made of wool. Quite often they

ILLUSTRATION 101.

were a part of the wedding costume.

One beautiful shawl (see Ill. 99) had a motif of
the "paisley" design: teardrop, scroll, and medal-
lion, inspired from Persian ornament. This particular shawl, from the trousseau of Sarah Maria
Meigs, married in 1838, was 130 inches long, 64
inches wide, and had a four-and-a-half-inch border at either end. It had a black-patterned center,
eleven inches in diameter, and a green selvage.
Another wool Paisley shawl, sixty-five inches
square and fringed at the ends, had Hindu motifs
(see Ill. 100). In teardrop, fanspread, and loop
pattern it was made in red, rose, gold, and gray.
It belonged to a young woman who came from
Nottingham, England, traveled as a pioneer to
Manti, Utah, in 1853, and on to Ephraim in
1854. She was the first woman to be married
there.

Not all of the warm shawls bore a paisley pattern. Plaids, too, were favored, and sometimes
the wraps were homespun and plain. One fine
cashmere plaid shawl (see Ill. 101) had a blue
background with a one-inch dark blue stripe and
a two-inch brown stripe; it was a fringed square
with a fine, close weave. The shawl was presented

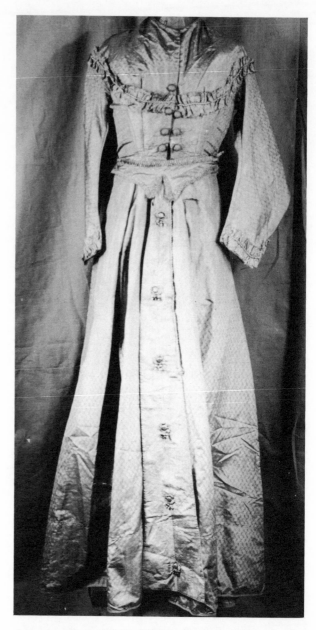

ILLUSTRATION 102. *An 1841 wedding dress without its separate belt and front panel.*

ILLUSTRATION 103. *The dress in Ill. 102, with its separate belt and front tapered panel with buttons.*

ILLUSTRATION 104. *Detail of the satin button with tassels.*

EMBROIDERY FOR CHEMISES.

INSERTING.

LADY'S HOOD.
(See description, page 92.)

ILLUSTRATION 105.

to a young bride on her wedding day in 1848, in Norway. It found its way to Utah in the hands of its proud owner.[35]

Not only were the shawls pretty possessions, but they were quite practical and were put to use in many ways. On cool evenings, which turned into cold nights, they kept many a couple warm. Many times the Paisley shawls were "family affairs." While still new and bright they were a wedding endowment; on special christening days, young mothers arrived with babies tucked warmly in the shawls. If aunts and cousins came to spend a few weeks, they were allowed to wear them to the church concert or social; and at night, if they were short of bedding, as a special

favor the shawl was laid across their feet. Even when a shawl became old and worn, it could be drawn across the tired shoulders of a loving grandmother.[36]

Capes, which served the same purpose as the neck-hugging shawls, were also plentiful and popular. Of note is a black satin cape lined in gray satin, cut in circular gores. The owner of the cape came across the plains around 1851 from Missouri. Upon arrival, she added to her cape a pleated grosgrain ribbon ruffled around the edges. She wore it on July 24, 1858, her wedding day.[37]

When one lived in the undeveloped frontier, courtship and marriage were a little bit of happiness sandwiched in between long days of hard labor on the land. In the southwestern territories, newcomers witnessed a truly bizarre landscape, which swept down from pine-covered mountain to arid desert. Those who were seeking a permanent home had much to learn about taming this wilderness.

Between 1847 and 1851, no serious attempts were made to farm the country beyond the Missouri River. Mining was the main pursuit. Men were miners, explorers, prospectors, or traders. Restlessness eventually gave way to homesteading. Some went west to avail themselves of public grants of land. The women who went with these able-bodied men helped to fence in the vast acres of rugged terrain.

A young bride had considerable work just to make ends meet, especially regarding her clothing. Her wedding dress, made of calico, linen, or wool, was used until it was completely worn out. Dresses were plain, with pockets sewn into the seams to take the place of handbags. Nearly every woman who came west had made provision for future needs and had brought along some lengths

ILLUSTRATION 106.

In 1864, a sixteen-year-old girl accompanied a party of pioneers to a sparsely populated section of the Southwest and settled among friendly Indians. She was married in July 1865. Her dress was of blue silk mohair (which she had brought with her), with little pinpoint snowflakes in it. The sleeves were leg-of-mutton style. There were six widths of the silk in the skirt, and a set of hoops was worn under it. Her hair was long and black; for the ceremony, an Indian squaw had waved and braided it for her, placing a comb upright in front like a crown. The comb, black with little gold prongs, matched her earrings, which had little sets of gold in the center, and the bracelets on each wrist. She wore a smaller comb in back, over which was arranged a black shawl with small beads of gold at the corners.

The bride's husband-to-be was a shoemaker. His special present to her was a handmade pair of shoes constructed of the tops of an Indian fighter's boots. She declared these to be the most comfortable shoes she had ever worn in her life. She had small hands and feet and weighed only ninety-two pounds. Before sunrise the next morning, a brass band from a neighboring town drove up to their adobe house serenading them, in the custom of welcoming a bride and groom to married life. The husband thanked the players and treated them all to a glass of Dixie wine.[40]

The 1841 wedding dress in Illustrations 102, 103, and 104 is a lavender pinstripe on gray silk with a small all-over leaf design. In the style of the 1840s, it had the dropped shoulder and long sleeves. The deep yoke was trimmed with a double ruffle, pinked at the edges with a cord of silk in the center. Satin buttons with tassels added a decorative feature.

Arizona was practically unknown to white settlers until well after the beginning of U.S. rule,

of fine materials. One young pioneer brought with her an organdy dress, but she was killed on the plains in an accident before she could wear it. Another woman, coming from England in 1854, brought a heavy silk gown of a claret color with her.[38]

In many instances a wedding dress was passed on to another woman for her wedding. One girl of fifteen needed a dress for her marriage, and a fifty-year-old neighbor of portly size lent her a dress of bombazine, which was stiff and harsh. It had to be pinned up in several places to fit, but the girl was nonetheless delighted to have something new. One satin dress was treasured by its owner, but she gave it up graciously when it was needed to line a casket and make a burial gown.[39]

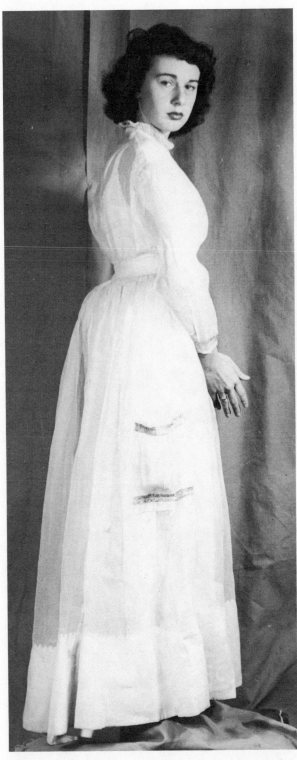

ILLUSTRATION 107. *A white organdy dress with pink trim of embroidered organdy and pink silk ribbon was worn by a bride in 1878 in Santa Clara, Utah. The one-piece dress had a high neckline finished with one-inch ruching of embroidered organdy. The full, gathered skirt had a large pocket of gathered organdy on the outside, trimmed with pink knife-pleated ribbon at top and bottom.*

except for a very limited and intermittent missionary effort. A few heroic explorers and Franciscan friars from Mexico came to this hostile land, but most homesteaders moved on to greener valleys. Still, eventually some permanent homes were established in the long vistas of desert and canyon.

Two young Pennsylvanians—a lawyer and Civil War veteran, and a schoolteacher who had spent her girlhood on a farm near Meadville, north of Pittsburgh—had a July wedding in 1868. Ill health made the husband seek the Arizona desert, so in 1871, he made his way to Tucson. The following year his wife joined him. Their names, as it turned out, were destined to head the list of Arizona's notables and patriots. Louis C. Hughes became the fiery publisher of the *Arizona Daily Star* and served as territorial governor when the state's capital was in Tucson. Josephine Brawley Hughes, his wife, won the hearts of the people of Old Pueblo with her civic works and with the hardiness known only to frontier women.

For the young bride, the journey from Meadville to Tucson was a saga of courage. She had to make the trip by rail to San Francisco, then by steamer to San Diego, and finally travel the 500 miles to Tucson by stagecoach, carrying her baby daughter in her arms. This journey was undertaken without the security and companionship of her new husband. The established, substantial Pennsylvania town she had left made a sharp contrast to the crude village of San Diego, with its rough dirt streets and shacks. Then she faced the last leg of the trip—into Apache desert country.

Wrapped in her linen duster, she boarded the stage with her baby and a few other passengers for the overland ride. For five days and nights the stage floundered over the rough roads. Through

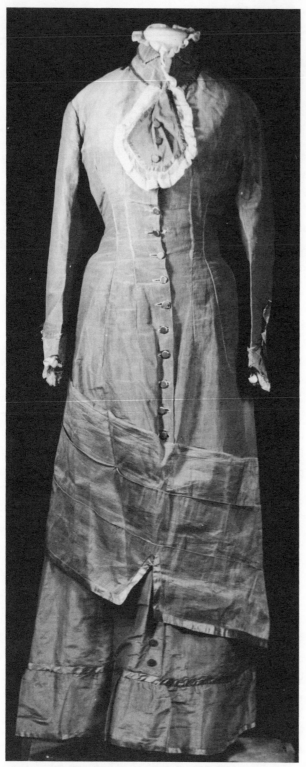
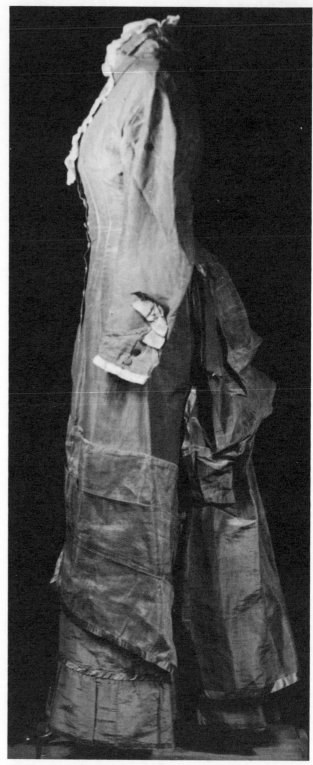

ILLUSTRATIONS 108 & 109. *A gray poplin dress in the style of the 1870s was made by the bride's mother and a friend for an August wedding in 1879 in Sandy, Utah. The dress was princess style with an asymmetrical line, the style of this period. The overskirt separated in the back to give emphasis to the* *bustle, which fell in three puffs or loops down the back; this was headed by three satin buttons and two ribbon bows. The neckline had a high stand-up collar and a seven-inch jabot. Neckline and jabot were edged with lace and organdy. Gray satin-covered buttons ornamented the front.*

ILLUSTRATION 110.

ILLUSTRATION 111. *Pink satin was chosen for this wedding dress. It is a gored princess style with bodice and shaped overdrape at the hips. There are twelve white satin buttons down the front and lace trimming from shoulder to waistline. The skirt has three bias folds around the bottom and is gathered in a puff over the bustle in the back.*

canyons, over mountains, miring in mud, ferrying the Colorado River, and then crossing the hot desert, the stage traveled. It stopped only briefly to change horses at stage stations. (Passengers traveling through Arizona Apache country were furnished an armed escort by the government to protect them and the mail. Members of a tribe had ravaged those passing on the road just twenty-four hours before and then had gone on their way.) Through many miles of desert, clouds of dust swirled around the stage, obliterating any view. Josephine's duster was ineffective as protection; dust filtered to her skin. She wondered whether the baby's chances of survival would be better breathing the dust or smothering under a hot blanket.

At last, worn, bruised, and battered, this young pioneer bride reached Tucson. She bravely faced the conditions of squalor in the small adobe village. The huts were grouped within the old Mexican presidio wall, where the inhabitants were Papago and Pima Indians, Mexicans, people of mixed race, and many others. Although the area was hot, treeless, and bare, the young husband and his bride remained. Josephine was the third American woman to make her home in Arizona.[41]

Weather always played an important role in the lives of pioneers. If bitter cold or a heavy snowstorm came on a wedding day in the 1860s, the bride would have been warm and comfortable in a hood like the one pictured in Illustration 105. One bride, in 1862, prided herself on wearing a tiny bonnet, similar to a half-hat. It was made of silk faille, lace, and flowers, with beads attached.

A description of one bridal gown comes from *The Weekly Star,* November 8, 1877. The groom, one of Tucson's most prominent citizens, was part owner of the firm that mined the rich native copper from the Arivaipa Canyon. The bride wore a light blue silk gown; her bridal veil was suspended from the head ornament of a wreath of white flowers.

In an adobe residence on South Main Street in Tucson, Arizona, a young girl from Sutter Creek, Amador County, California, wed one of Tucson's early pioneers and prominent citizens (see Ill. 106). The residence was the home of the bride's uncle and aunt. The wedding took place on Sunday evening, June 29, 1879, in the yard. The beautiful Hebrew ceremony, at which a large number of friends of both bride and groom were present, was completely described in *The Arizona Star* on July 1, 1879. It was the first Jewish marriage to take place in the Arizona Territory.

A waist of checked nainsook with pearl buttons and a skirt (see Illustration 110) of striped nainsook composed the bridal costume of a seventeen-year-old bride. She was the daughter of pioneers; her father came from England and her mother from Prussia in the early 1860s. Her wedding took place in 1880.

To the pioneers, whether their destination was America's West, Northwest, or Southwest, the wedding dress was the prized article of apparel. If it did not survive the years intact, it was preserved in memory and description, passed on from daughter to daughter down through the generations.

7

Wedding Fashions
in Paintings and Illustrations

In homes throughout our country, pastel portraits, oil paintings, and watercolors hang on
walls, some fondly cherished for many generations. Among them are portraits of a bride or her
bridal party, and these works of art give us the
truest picture of what was actually worn on wedding days of the past. Long before the camera
recorded her, artists spent hours faithfully depicting the bride in her finery. Some of the best
examples are found in museums.

A charming painting, *A Quaker Wedding*
(1820) by Percy Bigland, portrays the Empire
style of dress at the time. The bride, dressed in
simple fashion, wore the Quaker bonnet. A study
of *The Sailor's Wedding,* by Richard Caton Wood-
ville, gives an engaging glimpse of the hour important to a bride and groom. The details of this

ILLUSTRATION 113.

ILLUSTRATION 112.

colorful oil painting tell a story and the artist has beautifully portrayed the bride's dress (see Ill. 112).

In more recent times it is the illustrator, as well as the painter of fine arts, who enjoys drawing and painting the one costume set apart from a woman's wardrobe. Wedding finery provides good material for capturing a special day in illustration, fine art, or photography.

Charles Dana Gibson gave us the "Gibson Girl" model, but other artists, such as Harrison

Fisher, popular illustrator of the early twentieth century, enjoyed portraying her, too.

In March 1905, the center pages of the *Ladies' Home Journal* showed Harrison Fisher's drawing of a bride (see Ill. 113). His paintings also graced many magazine covers (see Ill. 114 and 115). Howard Chandler Christy, another very popular illustrator, used the bride as subject for several magazine covers (see Ill. 116).

The wedding subject popped up in another form of illustration: the picture postcard. Here,

THE GIRLS' MID-MAY NUMBER
THE LADIES' HOME JOURNAL

MAY 15, 1911

10 CENTS

PAINTED BY HARRISON FISHER
THE CURTIS PUBLISHING COMPANY, PHILADELPHIA

Copyright, 1911 (Trade-Mark Registered), by The Curtis Publishing Company, in the United States and Great Britain.   London: 6, Henrietta Street, Covent Garden, W. C.

ILLUSTRATION 114.

THE LADIES' HOME JOURNAL

OCTOBER 1913 · FIFTEEN CENTS

THE CURTIS PUBLISHING
COMPANY·PHILADELPHIA

PAINTED BY HARRISON FISHER

ILLUSTRATION 115.

THE BRIDAL NUMBER OF
THE LADIES' HOME JOURNAL

THE CHRISTY GIRL AS A BRIDE, AS DRAWN BY MR. HOWARD CHANDLER CHRISTY

MARCH 1905   FIFTEEN CENTS

THE CURTIS PUBLISHING COMPANY, PHILADELPHIA

ILLUSTRATION 116.

ILLUSTRATION 118.

WHEN IT COMES TO THE MORE SERIOUS BUSINESS OF LIFE, THIS YOUNG MAN SHOULD BE THE LAST TO
BLAME HER FOR EXERCISING A LITTLE FORETHOUGHT.

ILLUSTRATION 117. *A Charles Dana Gibson illustration of 1894.*

in a different version of wedded bliss, the bride
was drawn (see Ill. 118). The bride or groom
often took the brunt of a joke, like a dirty valentine.* Sometimes whimsey mixed with innocence—the cupid image and the Kewpie doll.
Often pure sentimentality and idealism were portrayed.

*People in the 1920s and 30s sent insulting valentines anony-
mously; these were called "dirty valentines" and were a popular
joke.

8

My Name is Isabella Jane; the Crinoline (Extravagant) Period (1850s and 1860s)

The middle of the nineteenth century was one of its most colorful periods. The transition from the former style, as women piled on more and more petticoats and the skirt became voluminous, will be seen clearly in this chapter.

Two things occurred during these decades to excite public curiosity. One was part fad and part fantasy; the other was a foretoken of great industry. Both were within woman's domain.

In 1846, a machinist from Massachusetts named Elias Howe patented the first sewing machine. But introducing his new invention proved nearly impossible. Abroad, others had also worked to invent and produce a successful machine. Finally, in 1851, Isaac Merritt Singer marketed the first practical sewing machine, produced in a small shop in Boston. This did not

mean women could immediately begin sewing clothes by machine. It was a number of years until the sewing machine reached the American home, once it had been proved and tested. And even when machines made it into homes, it was some time before they were used regularly.

The other fashion event of the time was the increasing size of women's skirts. Ten yards of material were often barely enough fabric for the skirt alone! This led to the invention of the cage crinoline—the hoopskirt. (This is discussed later in the chapter, for in the early part of the decade women's clothing still reflected the feminine, demure look of the 1840s.) After skirts widened to their extreme, the dome shape, they began to diminish and narrow.

Two bridal costumes came to the public's view

ILLUSTRATIONS 119 - 121. *The Pennsylvania girl who wore this dress was married in May 1850. The bodice was boned and covered with sheer gauze to the high neckline, which was finished with lace. Thirty-four satin buttons covered with crochet were laced together at the back closing. The bride also wore a charming poke bonnet.*

ILLUSTRATION 122. *Detail of the delicate lace at sleeve edging.*

ILLUSTRATION 123.

from the pages of March 1850's *Godey's Lady's Book and Magazine*. The fashion plate in Illustration 123 described the gown on the right as "suitable to a tall and stately woman." The dress was of satin with five full flounces and a double bertha collar of a light French lace, styled *point d'appliqué*. The wreath of orange flowers and the tulle veil were set on a small cap that fitted the head closely. The gown on the left was a rich robe of *soie d'antique,* a very heavy, old-fashioned silk. The richness of the material required a plain

style, but it was ornamented with natural, full-blown white roses with their foliage, graduated in size from the hem to buds at the waist. The bodice and neckline were finished by a finely pleated chemisette* close to the throat. The veil, low in the forehead, was fastened back by bouquets of rosebuds at each side.

The two-piece tan ribbed silk dress in Illustration 124, worn at a June 1851 wedding in Brook-

*A vestee or dickey, generally sleeveless and made of fine cotton and lace or net, used primarily to fill low necklines.

ILLUSTRATION 124.

lyn, necessitated the wearing of many petticoats, including some starched ones. It is a pretty style with a long, pointed, boned bodice, bell-shaped sleeves lined with white taffeta, and a full skirt trimmed with fringed self-ruching and ruffles.

The three-piece off-white bengaline costume in Illustration 125 has similar styling as the tan ribbed silk in Illustration 124. Its long, full, bell-shaped sleeves had deep slits, accented with white, embroidered lawn undersleeves. The bodice had a center front opening with prominent crocheted buttons. The skirt, full and gored, was gathered in the back and had a long train. The wide self-belt had two bengaline rosettes. With the costume are bengaline ankle boots with side lacing.

Another gown of the early decade was made of white ribbed silk with flower sprays. The 1852 bride also wore a beautiful white silk fringed shawl with wide stripes of plain cloth alternating

ILLUSTRATION 125.

with the flowered pattern.

In the early years of the 1850s, a woman was encumbered with underclothing as well as weighty outer garments. She usually wore long, lace-trimmed drawers, a flannel petticoat, an underpetticoat, which was three and a half yards wide, a petticoat padded to the knees, the upper part stiffened with whalebones spaced eight inches apart, a white starched petticoat (often with three stiffly starched flounces), two muslin petticoats—and finally the dress.[42]

The bride who wore the elaborate brocade dress in Illustration 126 (c. 1855–60) was the daughter of a New Haven, Connecticut, industrialist who had the first canning factory there. The groom was a German who had a clothing store in New Haven. The handsome gown was a light tan and blue brocade with a full pleated skirt. The bodice

ILLUSTRATION 126.

the gathered, bouffant skirt, the bodice was sewn to the skirt with very small measurement at the dipped waistline, widening out to a low, round neckline. There was a drawstring at the neckline. The boned bodice had fifteen lacings in the back and tiny puffed sleeves.

The number of "underpinnings" in the many petticoats became a real encumbrance. But relief from the burden of sustaining all this weight came around 1856, with the invention of a cagelike frame. This lightweight hoopskirt consisted of about twenty light steel wires (hoops), held together by strips of muslin or tape. The exaggerated, expansive dress pushed women, previously unnoticed in a very male world, into the limelight.

Curiously, the voluminous skirt falling from a tiny waist accentuated the feminine psyche; it satisfied a striving for exclusiveness in the social ladder. Most women thoroughly enjoyed wearing the absurd hoop, which swayed from side to side so alluringly. There was a lure to the wearing of the hoop skirt, a feeling of moving dramatically in it, of power and flirtation—even for the bride.

had a low, pointed waist with hooks in front; it was trimmed with blue silk and chenille fringe. There were wide, flowing sleeves below the deep bertha collar.

In the 1854 dress in Illustration 129, the lightweight material spoke for itself in terms of elegance. The material was a horizontal stripe of silk taffeta and satin. In order to give full play to

ILLUSTRATION 127. *For a June wedding in 1854, this lightweight silk brocade dress was made with a very full, gathered skirt and a boned bodice. The entire dress was lined, and bust pads were sewn in. The sleeves, which were very short, were bordered with silk wire braid.*

ILLUSTRATION 128. *The design of the brocade of dress in Ill. 127. Delicate in appearance, the fabric had a French-style design of garlands of small flowers and leaves. A plain gold wedding band was preserved with this dress. Rounded on the outside, flat against the finger, it was inscribed: J. C. STOVER/ M.E.C./ JUNE 28, 1854.*

ILLUSTRATION 128.

ILLUSTRATION 127.

ILLUSTRATION 129.

ILLUSTRATION 130. *Back view of a dress worn by a Delaware bride at her 1854 wedding.*

ILLUSTRATION 131.

She could lean too close to the altar rail, tipping up the hoopskirt in back to reveal those lacy undergarments. Walking down the aisle, she could not even take her husband's arm, could barely touch his shoulder at full arm's length, because she and her attendants needed a great amount of space in which to maneuver.

Under the Second Empire, France displayed an ostentatious style of dress imaginable only in an era of affluence and extravagance. After Louis Napoleon married Spanish beauty Eugenie Marie (see Ill. 131) on January 29, 1852, the new empress soon created the most brilliant court in Europe. By her beauty and accomplishments she drew to her the fashion of the world. Just as her husband was dictator of affairs, she became the dictator of all refinement.

The imperial regime expected Eugenie to be a power in the state, attracting attention and admiration. This expectation she fulfilled in the highest measure; no one could ever complain that the court had a dearth of fashionable splendor and imperial brilliance.

If there was an excess of fashion, there was also an excess of extravagance around the court of Eugenie, which affected first the high life of Paris, then the whole of French society, and ultimately the world.[43] Naturally, young American women were influenced by this enchanting empress. She was the first to wear the expansive crinoline, for example, and other women followed her lead.

The very full, dome-shaped skirt—the crinoline cage—enjoyed its height of popularity from 1858 to 1860, but it was still loved and worn in 1861 by women from the highest rungs of society to working women and even milkmaids.

One lovely dress, worn in December 1858, is still in excellent condition tody. It is a brown plaid of shot-silk taffeta with handsome pagoda sleeves, scalloped and fringed, and a detachable bertha collar, also fringed. Most likely, there were separate undersleeves. Much is known about the bride who wore this beautiful dress at her wedding on Christmas Eve in 1858. Her story, in her own words, follows.

My Name Is Isabella Jane

The festivities are now over, and I wish to tell you about the happy days surrounding Christmas (our Weinachtsfest), and our wedding celebration. It was a bit different

ILLUSTRATION 133. *Detail of the pagoda sleeve on Isabella's dress.*

ILLUSTRATION 132. *Isabella's dress.*

ILLUSTRATION 135. *Isabella's wedding announcement*.

ILLUSTRATION 134. *Isabella's cloak and bonnet*.

this year of 1858 and ever so joyous; for George and I were married Christmas Eve.

There were months of preparation; the candle-making began first. That we did in the summer months. When the hot summer days were near an end, and cooler evenings signaled an early fall, Mother and I chose a clear, early morning to drive down to Harrisburg to see the styles and buy some pretty material for my wedding dress. We hitched our favorite horse to the buggy and took the three-hour drive along the Susquehanna River to town. We considered ourselves fortunate to find a suitable hitching post in the square. Mother wore a green dress with full crinoline hoop, and mine was my favorite gray silk with cords and buttons of deep blue. (It was not my Sunday best.) We had quite a time maneuvering our hoopskirts in the buggy.

The stores were still showing mostly summer dresses, but a few fall and winter bolts of handsome silks and taffeta plaids were shown to us. Brown silk plaids were very popular last year, and this year, too. I selected one of these. This material is beautiful over the hoops, and my plaid design has white and red, as well as the browns. My dress would use sixteen yards of material. For trimming, I found the exact colors in braid fringe needed to harmonize—brown and green—it had just come from New York. Our purchases included the brown velvet and black passementerie* braid for the cloak and bonnet.

We were sure to include thread, lining

*Applied trimmings such as braid, cords, and heavy embroideries.

ILLUSTRATION 136. *This black silk taffeta dress of 1860 had a side-front opening placket.*

material, hooks and eyes, pins and needles with our purchases, for we did not drive to town as often as father did, and it was well to be supplied.

One accessory I was anxious to buy was a small bunch of artificial flowers—they are new, and so popular; I bought ones like roses, but in warm, rosy colors. I arranged them along with the holly from our garden, into a small nosegay.

Happy hours were spent during the colorful fall season, although the news which father, uncle or the boys brought from the city was disturbing. Hostility was reported between the States, and an actual war threatened, despite all efforts to dispel the differences.

My dear friend, Mattie, who was married last month in Philadelphia, wrote about the fashionable society in which she travels and what was expected of her. How lucky I am that mine is a much narrower circle of friends in country life; my way of living is more peaceful and domestic.

Mattie said that even her friends were expected to prepare for her wedding. Her morning receptions required almost a full dress toilet! The dresses themselves were rich and light, the scarves and cashmere shawls extremely elegant. One bonnet was of white terry velvet with a small plume of white feathers on one side, the under-brimming of blonde and white roses and strings of white terry velvet ribbon. There were evening receptions for Mattie and of course, the wedding ball, which was the prelude to several of the large parties. The gowns sounded so beautiful! Striped silks and taffetas, deep blue, purple and maroon figured with black velvet.[44] I love my wardrobe but my dresses seem plain next to city clothes. Mother and I worked hard all those months to make my new wardrobe, with the help of Bertha, who is an excellent seamstress.

So much activity heightened the excitement of the holidays and our plans for the wedding as the month of December hastened to an end. We baked cookies of all kinds two to three weeks before the wedding and I could not describe the many other good foods we prepared.

The day of the wedding was a crisp and snowy day. The deep snow made it impossible for friends from far away to come, even from Harrisburg; but we had family and friends from nearby farms who came in sleighs. Thankfully, the Reverend Rieffer was able to come.

The ceremony was set for six o'clock. Mother and I made sure all the rooms in the house would be warm enough for our guests in this bitter weather; all the spare rooms were opened, with candle-stands and candle-holders ready. We supplied all the fireplaces with fragrant wood. The parlor looked lovely with all the candles and there was a great waft of fragrance from the evergreens we had brought in.

Altogether, it was the most exciting and wonderful day!

Black Wedding Dresses

There may be those who imagine that the black wedding dress was rare. Not at all! Throughout the nineteenth century, black was the conventional wedding color for a number of cultures; many Germans, Poles, and people from Slavic countries sported black marital garb. A black suit or traveling costume was a practical and chic garment. (My own Pennsylvania grandmother, of German descent, wore a two-piece black suit with a bustle when she was married in 1887.) Brides in mourning for a parent or close relative also wore black.

In the 1930s there appeared a vogue for wearing sleek black satin wedding dresses and carrying calla lilies. (See Chapter 15.)

Illustration 137 shows the foundation garments, bridal dress, and veil of a bride of 1860.

ILLUSTRATION 137.

ILLUSTRATION 138.

ILLUSTRATION 139. *Back view of the dress in Ill. 138.*

She was suitably dressed in a linen chemise trimmed with embroidery and lace, and drawers, which had rows of tucks and eyelet lace at the knee. She wore white silk stockings with cotton tops and shaping in the legs. Her satin boots had side lacing. The corset was short on the hips, dipping in front. The camisole was worn over the corset. The crinoline hoopskirt of nine hoops of watch spring was incorporated into the petticoat. A hoopskirt similar in style is described in Chapter 12.

The bridal dress of this costume is a gored, princess style made of sixteen yards of thick white silk; the only ornaments are flat white bows of satin ribbon fastened by pearl buckles in the center. These bows extend from the throat to the hem of the skirt. A large cuff of lace decorates the long sleeve above the wristband. The veil is of tulle; the wreath, mounted in coronet form, is made of small flowers, jessamine, and rosebuds.[45]

Plaid silk taffeta wedding dresses were favored over the solid color or white. One hand-sewn silk taffeta dress (see Ill. 138) has a beautiful plaid, with a fine horizontal print and a vertical stripe of watered moiré in a small, colored motif. The full hooped skirt has a large box pleat in center front, then small inverted box pleats around the skirt. The upper bell sleeve is separate from the lower and is made with a braided cord lacing. The undersleeve is of sheer dotted net cuffed with tiers of inset lace and lace edging. A brocade loop fringe trims the bodice and sleeves; the bodice has two crocheted, tasseled rosette buttons. The young bride was twenty years old when she made

ILLUSTRATION 140.

the dress for her wedding, in October 1860.

Only in time of great prosperity and affluence can one use so many yards of material for each costume, particularly when making plaids, which had to be matched. An Alabama girl chose a plaid of blue and gold shot-silk taffeta for her December 1860 wedding (see Ill. 140). With low bateau neckline and short gathered sleeves, the dress had a matching shawl or bertha, trimmed with ribbon. Separate sleeve inserts, created in pagoda-sleeve style, made it more comfortable for the winter.

A steel engraved fashion plate (see Ill. 141) for December 1861, from *Godey's Lady's Book,* speaks

ILLUSTRATION 141.

for itself. The first figure shows a very costly lace gown, but the dresses that follow contrast it with their marked simplicity.

Hoopskirts and crinolines were once again favored in the 1950s, particularly the end of the decade. Tiny waistlines and tiny headpieces let the eye take in the bouffant skirt and the pretty bustline. One chapel gown at the end of the decade had a nine-tiered skirt with a brief train, a Sabrina neckline, and a bodice scattered with iridescent sequins and pearls. The pearl headpiece holding the short veil was called "the double cupcake."

America in 1860 was doing what it still loves to do—putting out a red carpet for visiting dig-nitaries, staging parades, and entertaining on a grand scale. In October 1860, a gala ball was given in New York City for the Prince of Wales, Queen Victoria's eighteen-year-old son. He was honored and fêted at the Academy of Music on Fourteenth Street, where a ballroom was constructed. Four thousand invitations were sent out. Each lady wore her loveliest crinoline and ball gown—in fact the floor had to be measured to allow a five-foot circle for each lady's crinoline petticoat! Besides the guests, there were sumptuous decorations, and in the crush of hoopskirted dancers, large vases of roses and gladioli were knocked to the floor. Even so, the ball was a grand success.[46]

ILLUSTRATION 142. *This brown velvet wedding dress was brought from the East to Michigan in 1863. Max Unger's watercolor rendering of this dress is a faithful copy.*

Thinking big and doing things with flair became common practice. Weddings, too, assumed mammoth proportions. All the extravagances of women's clothes and the flaunting of material wealth belied the symptoms of strife that ultimately caused the Civil War.

We think of the antebellum South as a romantic time, with lovely brides from plantation homes marrying in resplendent hooped wedding gowns. In fact, clothing of the Civil War years is scarce, a poignant reminder of the devastation that took place during that time. Sherman's march through Georgia left a trail of destruction, including complete wardrobes, fine clothing, accessories and, of course, wedding dresses.

One young girl, Fanny Green, who was to be

ILLUSTRATION 143.

ILLUSTRATION 144. *This style required puffed tulle over a silk underskirt and a tunic of silk with flowing sleeves.*

ILLUSTRATION 145. *This satin dress has an overdress of point lace, with the popular looped-up overskirt. Some overskirts of the day were drawn up like paniers.*

married during wartime, had a harrowing experience. New Orleans had fallen, and families had assembled all their most precious worldly goods, preparing to flee if their homes were destroyed.

Captain Green himself rushed back home to announce the ultimatum to his family: evacuation within a day. A Methodist preacher was summoned; messengers were hastily sent to a few neighbors, asking their presence that afternoon at the marriage of his daughter. Kind neighbors came early, helping the distracted girls to pack. Every room of the big house had trunks, boxes,

bags, baskets, and barrels, piles and piles of household and personal articles to be stowed. Everybody was busy, tearing about, getting in one another's way.

It was agreed: Fanny must be married in white. Trunks and drawers were ransacked for a pretty white lawn dress she had—somewhere! Finally, it emerged in very crumpled condition, not having been worn since the last winter that Fanny had spent in Washington with her father. There was no time, opportunity, or place to press the wrinkles out and make the really handsome gown

ILLUSTRATION 146. *A brown taffeta (1865) has a short peplum, which extends the bodice and fits smoothly over the hips. The dress was altered in the 1870s.*

presentable. Added to this was a frantic search for white stockings. Nobody had the temerity to mention white kid gloves. They were of the past, as completely as a thousand other necessities they would have to learn to do without.

Fanny, lovely in her white gown, was the most calm and composed of any of them. The dazed, wounded Captain meandered around in his dingy Confederate gray, the only suit he had. Time was passing more quickly than the little party could believe. All the packing and loading of the wagons had to be completed for the early-morning start. A part of the company stayed in their homes to take their chances. But Captain

Green's girls had to be off, in accordance with his dictum; a Confederate officer had to get out of reach of the enemy.[47]

So much could be told about the brides of the Civil War. Like the pioneer women who crossed the plains with their new husbands, these women adapted to completely alien and unexpected conditions. But in the midst of enormous turmoil, little things still could matter. A bride, unable to buy hairpins, would use thorns to secure her "waterfall" hair arrangement (later called a chignon).

The purple dress in Illustration 143 was worn by a Roxborough, Pennsylvania, judge's daughter in 1865. Purple denoted mourning for the bride's father, a colonel in the Civil War, killed while commanding his Pennsylvania regiment. The dress was a handsome taffeta, trimmed with matching, figured taffeta with white and yellow design. The bodice had an off-the-shoulder neckline and a fitted body with elongated points at the front and back of the waistline. There were eight white ball buttons at the front closing. Around the entire skirt hem was a deep pleated ruffle of figured taffeta. White braid trimmed the ruffle head, as well as the shoulder, waist, and cuff.

A decided change in the silhouette emerges in these last two dresses (Ills. 144 and 145). The hoopskirt fashion had finally peaked. These two bridal fashions from 1868 show the direction the hoop was taking—sinking down to the hem.

Brown was a favorite color for wedding dresses before the Civil War, and afterward. It was seen in solid color and in plaid.

With a Worth & Bobergh label, the elegant ball gown in Illustration 147 was first a wedding dress. For the marriage ceremony (c. 1865) it had a more modest bodice. The creation is of nougat satin trimmed with tulle, swansdown, crystal

ILLUSTRATION 147.

beads, and glass pearls.

An 1870 dress of sheer cotton mull over a hoop can be seen in Illustration 150. It has an interesting sheer apron-style overskirt, vertically scalloped at the sides and caught up by three satin rosettes. This overskirt descends in the back to a semitrain. The bodice has short, puffed sleeves with long, flaring undersleeves. The yoke has ver-

tical satin bands and sheer ruching.

American economic life picked up rapidly after the war. The end of the decade witnessed a surprising industrial surge. What we recognize as the department store had its beginning during this period. Macy's, in New York, after small beginnings in 1858 in the form of a "fancy goods" shop, developed into the largest store in the

ILLUSTRATION 148. *A hooped silk-satin gown of 1864 with a cotton net under-bodice. The fullness of the sleeves was stitched down, creating rows of puffs.*

ILLUSTRATION 149. *This Quaker wedding dress, worn in Philadelphia in 1865, was made of sheer ivory wool. It had a cape, semicircular in cut. All trim—on the cape, dress, and belt rosette—was in the self-material of sheer wool.*

ILLUSTRATION 150.

world. At first selling only ribbons, laces, feathers, handkerchiefs, and ladies' gloves, it gradually added new lines and larger buildings.

Department stores were unknown in those days. The only other store in New York City that sold as many different kinds of items as Macy's (shoes, clothing, ribbons, dishes, furniture, and accessories) was Lord & Taylor's. In fact, the term "department store" wasn't used until the 1890s.[48] The development of these stores was an important step in creating a new image for America, one that said "prosperity."

9

Victorian Woman to the Gibson Girl, American Model (1870-1900)

An unbelievable number of hours went into the making of gowns worn in the 1870s. Whether made by hand, by dressmaker, by garment factory, or by house of fashion, work on a costume was detailed and precise. Surfaces were decorated with careful workmanship; edgings, such as scallops, pinked ruching, flounces, and braidings, took the finest practice of stichery.

Dresses of this period gave the bride a regal feeling, or one of being on stage. Beautiful, bustled dresses with long dramatic trains, fully complemented by accessories and careful, elaborate hairstyling, brought the bride very much into the limelight.

It is no wonder these sumptuous dresses were treasured and preserved. In fact, many of the gowns found in museums across the country are from this bustle period. Most of these gowns were from America's upper middle class—from homes where servants helped dress the ladies in the complicated articles of attire. Very special attention was given to the bridal gown, underclothing, and accessories, and there was no thought of discarding these costly creations.

Today, museums, historical societies, and fashion institutes are actively searching out the garments worn by the middle and lower classes as well, essential for a true picture of any society.

The cuirass basque* bodice of the costume in

*A cuirass is a jacket or bodice lined and boned to fit smoothly over the torso (originally part of defensive armor for the upper portion of the body). A basque is a shaped, jacketlike bodice, fit close to the body and often ending below the waist in a short peplum or skirt.

ILLUSTRATION 151. *This gown, made for a November wedding in 1870, typifies
the elegance and grace of the time. Cream colored with satin trim, its skirt and bodice
are separate. The skirt is bustled and full in the back, has a trained overskirt edged
with scallops and two shorter panels, also scalloped.*

ILLUSTRATION 152. *Bridal accessories complement the gown in Ill. 151: a fine white cotton petticoat, flounced and tucked with embroidered eyelet and ribbon; white satin slippers with a satin rosette in a multibow, five-star ornament of beads and braid with tassel; wrist-length white kid gloves; and the finely embossed wedding invitation.*

Illustration 157 had short sleeves. It was rounded in front, short on the hips, and laced in back from yoke to the long pointed end with eighteen laces. The neckline was finished with narrow pleating and net ruche trim. The skirt showing the new asymmetrical line had a demitrain formed by deep pleats over the bustle, finished with a folded bustle bow. Three narrow, knife-pleated flounces finished the bottom of the skirt. Two faille flounces edged the short sleeves. The fringe had satin threads and tiny glass beads.

A newspaper article in the *Dubuque Daily Herald,* December 8, 1874, described one of the most elaborate of society weddings:

ILLUSTRATION 154. *Back view of the dress in Ill. 153.*

ILLUSTRATION 153. *Beautiful in its subtle coloring, beige with slate-gray satin trim, this dress dates from the late 1860s. In design, it is quite similar to the gown in Ill. 151, with peplum effect, scallops edged with satin, and satin bands at the neckline. It is also a two-piece costume, with a separate belt.*

ILLUSTRATION 155. *A Boston bride wore this wedding dress in November 1870. It was of pale blue-gray taffeta with fitted bodice, buttoned in front; the eight ornate buttons were pale gold. The yoke and neck were trimmed with fringed, pleated white taffeta ruching and machine-made lace.*

Marriage of Miss Rebecca M. Wells
and
Mr. M. M. Ham
—A brilliant Assemblage—
Distinguished Guests
Magnificent Display of Presents
Handsome Toilets, Etc. . . .

The bride was "universally conceded to be one of the most popular, amiable, and lovely ladies in Dubuque society." She was dressed in an elegant robe of rich lavender silk, trimmed with trailing sprays of orange buds and blossoms. Her wreath of the same bridal flowers held a veil of fine white tulle. Her complete bridal outfit came from the hands of a very skillful modiste unexcelled in her profession. A monogram of the bride's and groom's initials, covered with moss and rosebuds, embellished the center of the church, and over all trailed a heavy garland of evergreens interspersed with lilies. The bridesmaids wore white, some with pink satin bodices and others with cherry. The mothers wore handsome black silks, with lace trimmings and pond lilies in their hair. The column described in detail the costumes of at least thirty distinguished ladies. Six hundred guests attended the reception from 5:00 o'clock until 8:00 in the drawing rooms. The paper also listed the gifts, including money, telling how much was given by whom![49]

Women's magazines in the 1870s showed very beautiful wedding fashions, elaborate in style, fabric, and detailing. The elegant white gown had its zenith in this decade. But underneath the encrustation of corsets, stays, heavy materials, and accessories, the woman's body was squeezed and distorted. Many a bride's fainting spell was caused by this binding armor. Yet although this subjugation is easy to disdain, the Victorian woman's greatest desire was to attain the look and feel of pure femininity. She was proud of her poise, her dramatic movements, her virgin purity. The white veil asserted that she was all of that.

Illustrations 163 and 164 show fashion plates from the pages of *Godey's Lady's Book* for the years 1872 and 1876. The bustle was high fashion at the time, expertly styled and presented to an admiring public. The December 1872 plate (Ill. 163) shows a bride's dress of heavy corded silk, the front covered by folds of narrow tulle and turquoise silk. The underskirt was trimmed with a ruffle bound by a band of turquoise silk. It had a court train, cut in points and bound in silk to match the ruffle, the points edged by Valenciennes lace. There were coat sleeves with open hanging sleeves, trimmed to correspond with the skirt. The August 1876 fashion plate (Ill. 164) shows a bride dressed in white silk. The dress had a basque bodice with puffs of illusion and pleatings of Valenciennes lace, trimmed with fringe. There was an overskirt in front, pleated at the sides with fringe and orange blossom trim.

Since it was felt that wedding gowns should

ILLUSTRATION 156. *A wedding dress in five parts was made and worn in Boston in 1873. It consisted of the underdress, overbodice, overskirt, separate trained overskirt, and belt. The underdress was of pale blue taffeta; the overgarments were of shirred and puffed white net and lace.*

Jos. G. Darlington & Co.

ILLUSTRATION 160. *Inside the neckline of the gown in Ill. 157 was sewn this white satin label tag, with woven letters in blue.*

ILLUSTRATION 157. *From a Philadelphia shop in 1875 comes this two-piece bustle dress of pale ivory silk faille, styled much like the French fashions of the day.*

ILLUSTRATION 158. *Front view of gown in Ill. 157, with asymmetrical line of fringe.*

ILLUSTRATION 159. *Back view of gown in Illustration 157.*

ILLUSTRATION 161. *Gold and pale green taffeta and damask gown (1879).*

ILLUSTRATION 162. *Three brides from* Harper's Bazar, *August 1870.*

emphasize modesty, bridal outfits often had a second bodice. This second bodice was usually more formal in style, with a low neckline and shorter sleeves, and could be worn with the skirt as a ball gown.

Illustrations 166 to 170 show an 1870 wedding outfit of cream faille and satin with two bodices. Pictured are the wedding basque bodice, front and back, the second bodice, the skirt, and the brocade panel. The skirt was undoubtedly worn over a hoopskirt with bustle, the current

fashion. A distinctive feature of the skirt is a narrow gold brocade panel down the front. There is a matching pair of high-button shoes of cream faille, size 4, with the bridal outfit.

Women of the early 1960s found the bustle pert and attractive. They called it butterfly pouf back, bustle with a peacock train, and other names. Designer Alfred Angelo showed some pretty and very bouffant skirts in 1961.

In the 1870s, American culture—music, architecture, painting, literature and costume—

ILLUSTRATION 163.

ILLUSTRATION 164.

ILLUSTRATION 165. Harper's Bazar (*January 10, 1874*) *featured this fashion plate of children playing with bride dolls with bustles.*

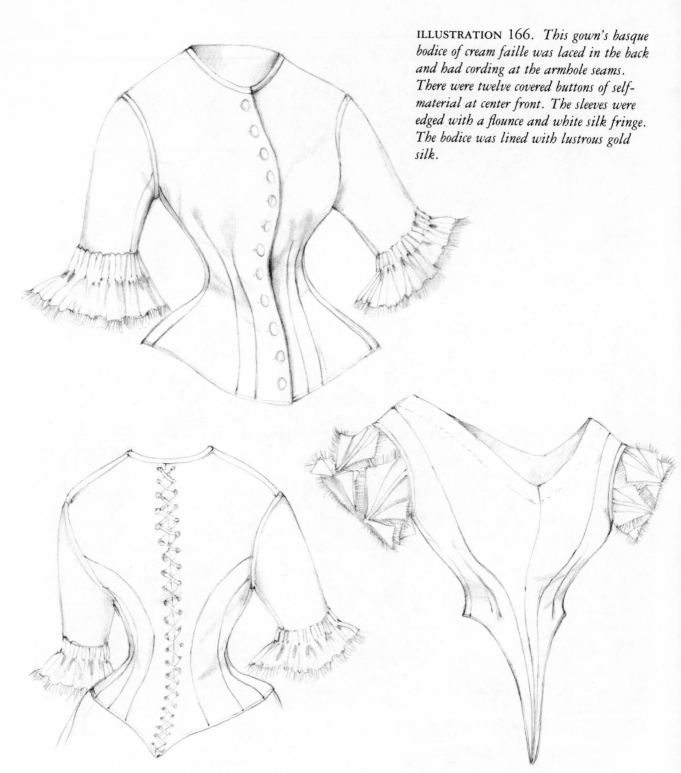

ILLUSTRATION 166. *This gown's basque bodice of cream faille was laced in the back and had cording at the armhole seams. There were twelve covered buttons of self-material at center front. The sleeves were edged with a flounce and white silk fringe. The bodice was lined with lustrous gold silk.*

ILLUSTRATION 167. *The back of the bodice of the gown in Ill. 166, showing twenty-one lacings down the center back.*

ILLUSTRATION 168. *The second bodice of the gown in Ill. 166 has very short sleeves with triple box pleats turned up in different lengths and edged with silk fringe.*

ILLUSTRATION 169. *The skirt front of the gown in Ill. 166, with gold brocade panel.*

ILLUSTRATION 170. *The skirt back of the gown in Ill. 166 is full, to accommodate hoopskirt and bustle.*

still reflected a strong influence from Europe. American painters such as John Singer Sargent and James A. McNeill Whistler went abroad and remained there. And particularly during the last three decades of the nineteenth century, the influence of the great European fashion designer Charles Frederick Worth cannot be denied (see Ill. 147 in Chapter 8). Many hampers of costumes and wedding dresses were sent to America—and all over the world—from the renowned House of Worth. One had a treasured garment of value if it had a Worth label.

ILLUSTRATION 171. *This regal wedding dress of gray taffeta with bustle and train was worn by the sister of Philadelphia's John Wanamaker at her wedding in October 1877.*

ILLUSTRATION 172. *This Worth gown (1878) was made of ivory and gold satin damask, trimmed with pearl appliqué and silk fringe.*

 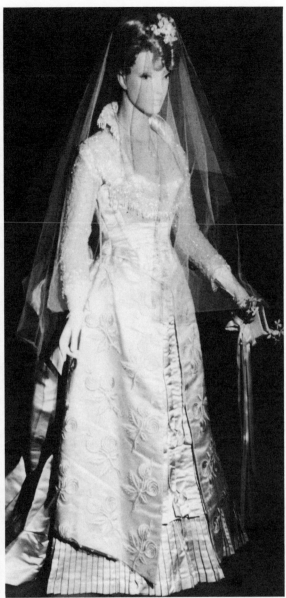

ILLUSTRATION 174. *The Montclair Art Museum has this wedding dress, worn in January 1880 by a direct descendant of Jasper Crane, in its costume collection. Crane was one of the founders of Newark, New Jersey, in 1666. His son settled Cranetown, now Montclair, New Jersey.*

ILLUSTRATION 175.

ILLUSTRATION 173. *This bustled dress of heavy white wool was worn at a spring 1880 wedding in Georgia. Daisies and fern in graduated green floss were on the left bodice front; sleeves and panel of the skirt were hand-embroidered.*

ILLUSTRATION 176. *An 1884 wedding gown of blue with darker blue brocade figures had a trained skirt and a dust ruffle with two panels of chenille trimming. The fitted basque bodice had a high collar and a front of lace and chenille. There were three-quarter-length sleeves.*

ILLUSTRATION 177. *This silk brocade bustle dress of 1885 was made by Lanouette, of New York and Paris.*

ILLUSTRATION 179.

ILLUSTRATION 180.

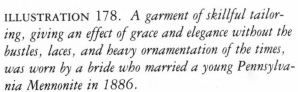

ILLUSTRATION 178. *A garment of skillful tailoring, giving an effect of grace and elegance without the bustles, laces, and heavy ornamentation of the times, was worn by a bride who married a young Pennsylvania Mennonite in 1886.*

ILLUSTRATION 181. *Seated here are a bride and the judge who performed her marriage ceremony in October 1887. The groom is standing. This wedding took place at the Cotton Exposition of 1887, at the Piedmont Expo.*

ILLUSTRATION 182. *In October 1888 a young Mexican woman living in Tucson married a civilian packmaster who had come to Arizona with the U.S. Army. The bride stood by her new husband's side in a bustled wedding dress; he was seated in the traditional pose of the decade.*

As a young English boy, Charles F. Worth went to Paris to seek his fortune and became one of the most influential and distinguished dress designers of all time. He won the patronage of the Empress Eugenie and, through her, of fashionable Paris. Although she brought him much of his fame, his own ingenuity and creativity were of the highest order. Features of the European court were incorporated into his designs. Ornate, long mantles, like robes of state, and ornate trains with ruffles and ruchings trailing behind became longer and fuller. Worth encouraged the silk weavers of Lyons, a source of gorgeous silks, to make a specially woven, lustrous white satin at his request. The lighter-weight satin was happily substituted for the heavier fabrics. Worth gowns from Paris were so special and costly that many were worn only once. That is why quite a few of them exist today in the finest condition possible.

Naturally, imported dresses from established

ILLUSTRATION 183.

ILLUSTRATION 185. *Magazines carried illustra-tions of hats made specifically for traveling brides.*

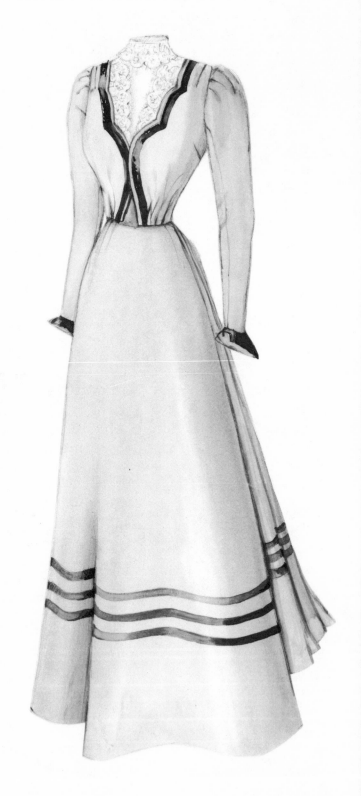

ILLUSTRATION 184.

ILLUSTRATION 186. *Two bunches of orange flowers pinned to this gown make a nice corsage. The gown was worn in April 1892.*

ILLUSTRATION 187.
A back view of the gown in Ill. 186.

ILLUSTRATION 188. *This portrait of a September 1891 bride shows a hairstyle popular in the early 1890s. In order to make the face appear small, the hair was swept up from the face, and ringlets were arranged on the forehead and at the nape of the neck.*

ILLUSTRATION 189. *From* Godey's Lady's Book, *January 1891.*

ILLUSTRATION 190. From Harper's Bazar, *1893.*

ILLUSTRATION 191.

ILLUSTRATION 192.

ILLUSTRATION 193. *This German couple was married in Austin, Texas, in August 1896. All the women in the wedding party wore the fashionable huge-sleeved gowns. The bride and groom's beautiful hand-colored* trau-schein *(marriage certificate) has been preserved (see Ill. 203).*

couturiers abroad were full of high-fashion splendor, especially in this period. With bows, ruffles, laces, jewels, fringes, pleatings and ribbons, clothing was almost frothy. The bride who made her own dress was not so lavish. New World creations were less elaborate, yet distinctive and lovely in their own way.

The main feature of the 1880 satin gown in Illustration 174 is the long, pointed bodice with side-front paniers, which were gathered and draped with deep fringe edging. From the deep point in the bodice back, the train was edged in cording and lace and had a fringed overtrain. The

skirt had panels of seven flounces of knife-pleating. This pleating was also at the elbow-length sleeve; there was ruching at the V-neck.

The 1883 satin gown in Illustration 175 was petite in size and very ornate in trimming and fabric. This gown had a low, square, décolleté neckline and a fitted bodice, pointed in front. The skirt, with heavy embroidered florals, was fashioned with a tablier* front rising in the back, where a huge satin bustle-bow trailed into a train

*An apron effect on a dress, popular from the late 1860s until the early 1880s.

ILLUSTRATION 194.

ILLUSTRATION 195.

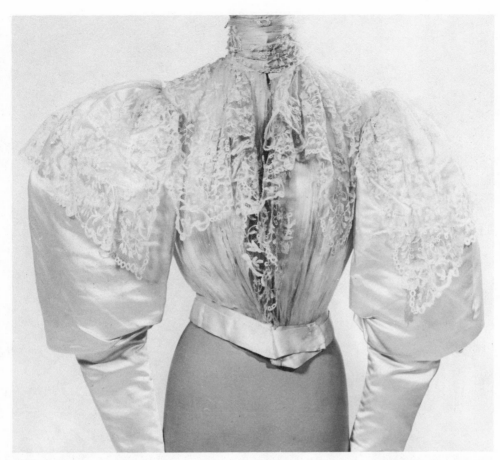

ILLUSTRATION 196. *Here, with its Paris label, is a white satin gown, showing the bodice alone. It is basically simple in design, but made elegant by the exquisite Rosepoint lace at the high neck, which covers the leg-of-mutton sleeves as well as the front of the bodice.*

padded and puffed with down or lamb's wool. The train itself was long and rounded, edged with fluting and two rows of lace showing beneath it. The dress had a glittering appearance, as the satin was embellished with embroidery, bugle beads, pearls, and fringe. There were long net sleeves, neckline, and collar (which was high and turned in back)—all embroidered in beads and pearls.

In this period there were also many attractive dresses in color. One plum-colored taffeta bustle dress had twenty distinctive buttons down the front of the long, pointed bodice. These buttons were metal, painted red, with a strawberry and leaf design.

In every period there are groups of people whose life-style and religious beliefs steer them to plain and simple living. They adapt the current fashions in a restrained and individual way. The result is pleasing and attractive.

Only a few early photographs of brides exist, but as the camera became more functional, we do find some fine bridal portraits. One young man, having immigrated to America from Germany, set up a photographic studio in a small town in Wisconsin. He met a young lady, who, he discovered, had also come from Germany and had lived less than fifteen kilometers from his home town. They married in America in 1888, the bride dressed in a black, two-piece bustle cos-

ILLUSTRATION 197. *Photograph entitled "The Wedding March" (1897).*

tume. Illustration 179 is the picture taken on their wedding day. The bride did not like the white veil and black basque combination, and a week later convinced her photographer-husband to have another picture taken (Ill. 180).

The return of the bustle in the 1880s had designers creating fashions that emphasized the hips in a complete camouflage of the natural form. Next, as fashion yearned for a new look at the end of the nineteenth century, the bustle was put aside for a focus on the shoulder and sleeve.

This does not mean to say that the corset was flung aside. Discipline continued to demand the tightly corseted waist and hourglass silhouette. Almost every bride was able to attain that tiny waistline figure, for sports were an important part of every woman's daily life. Cycling was one of the most popular sports, and many women's magazines had articles on how to ride, as well as how to dress. The woman cyclist had to wear gloves, keep her leggings buttoned, her hat pinned on securely, and wear a veil to keep her

ILLUSTRATION 198.

cipated, it was felt, neither the fulminations of the church nor the ridicule of the public had any effect on her. The divided skirt was not named "culotte" until later.

In the second half of the nineteenth century, brides in the East found that prestige came from ordering gowns from Paris. Western brides had special status if the gown was made by a modiste in one of the larger cities in the United States.

The 1890 bride in Illustration 183 must have looked most debonair in her robin's egg blue silk faille gown trimmed with white ostrich tips. The gown was made by a modiste in Kentucky for the wedding in Vernon, Texas. The bodice was pointed front and back, with front closing of twelve large hooks and eyes. The neck edge was trimmed with lace and white ostrich plumes, which followed down the entire bodice front and lower edge. Short puffed sleeves were cuffed with a gathered self-material, fringed, and a metallic gold braid with blue beads. Sleeves were finished with gathered lace. The bodice was heavily boned (fifteen steels) at seams and darts and was lined in blue sateen. A rosette-type gathering at the back of the neck was inset with braid and beads. The skirt followed the style of the period—full-pleated at the side front and a separate panel train in back; this could be removed to transform the dress into a ball gown.

Traveling Suits

In rural areas and small towns in the South particularly, brides often wore wedding suits, because after the ceremony the bride and groom traveled by train or steamer to distant cities.

A couple might be married at 6:30 P.M. after the celebrations of the day in a church, go home

hair neat.[50] Cycling was universal, practiced by everyone from queens of Europe to celebrities in America. Actresses Lillian Russell and Sarah Bernhardt worked off superfluous pounds by riding a bicycle daily.

Not everyone approved of the new fashion required for riding, however. The controversial divided skirt, which opened out into Turkish bloomers or trousers, started a scandal. Women who wore bloomers were threatened with denial of the sacraments; once a woman became eman-

after the ceremony to be congratulated by relatives and a few friends, then be driven to the train depot for an 8:15 train to scheduled cities. The bride might wear a two-piece myrtle green wool costume, as shown here in Illustration 184, worn in 1899; it's highly suitable for traveling. The sleeves and bodice of this suit were trimmed with brown velvet. The bodice was fitted, with a scalloped front opening and long, tight-fitting sleeves. The skirt was cut to train, with godets* in the back. Three rows of brown velvet decorated the skirt.

California brides often wore traveling suits. A wedding in San Diego on December 29, 1890, took place in a parlor under a carriage parasol lined with roses, with more roses twined around the staff and handle. The bride carried a bouquet of roses and wore a brown faille gown with a corsage band of orange blossoms. After the wedding the entire party drove to the steamer *Pomona,* bound for San Francisco.

On February 18, 1891, another wedding in San Diego was followed by a 4:00 P.M. train trip to San Francisco. The bride wore a traveling suit of navy blue ostrich bands, with a turban to match. Another bride, in April 1891, wore a blue-gray India silk and cream lisse suit with orange flowers and "bride" roses.[51]

About this time, the word *corsage* underwent a change in meaning. Formerly, *corsage* meant the bodice or the upper part of a woman's dress, also fabric draped over the rib cage. Now, corsage came to mean a bouquet of flowers, real or artificial, used to decorate a costume.

Illustrations 189 and 190, from 1891 and 1893 fashion books, clearly show the gradual development and enlarging of the upper sleeve to its fullest shape in around 1896–97.

A governor's daughter wore the thin, cream-

*Segments of cloth wider at the bottom, used as insets to produce fullness or for widening, as in a skirt.

ILLUSTRATION 199.

ILLUSTRATION 200. *This bride has an 1899 bridal veil topped with a bunch of feathers called a panache. This upright ornament of plumes was also sometimes called an aigrette.*

colored, crinkled crêpe dress in Illustration 191 at her wedding on June 30, 1891. It had a short waist with a side band of pearl trimming around the lower part of the shirred waist. The sleeves were full to the elbow. The full, gathered sheer material fell into a short graceful train from a point high in the center of the yoked back. (Gown by Barrett's of New York.)

Without question, the most fashionable wedding of this period was the wedding of Consuelo Vanderbilt, who became the Duchess of Marlborough on November 7, 1895. Held at high noon, it was a grand affair, with a preconcert by Walter Damrosch and a choral ensemble with organ.

The bride's dress was cream white satin. It had a full court train bordered with exquisite embroidery of opalescent leaves, seed pearls, and silver. The rich point-lace flouncing on the skirt was especially made from designs suggested by the bride's mother. Orange blossoms and a ruching of lace and chiffon embellished the bodice, which had a high lace stock. The long tulle veil was fastened with an arrangement of orange blossoms made to represent a coronet. Orchids, lilies of the valley, and fern from England made up her bouquet, which was tied with long satin streamers.

Everything in the bride's trousseau was embroidered with the ducal coronet and had been ordered by the dozen. A treatise could be written describing this trousseau, the jewels, diamonds, pearls, the fine accessories, and also the costly wedding gifts. The entire interior of St. Thomas Church was decorated with flowers and ferns, including hanging baskets of orchids sent from the greenhouses at Blenheim, England, the duke's home. Gates of flowers attended by a small boy were erected in front of each pew. The walls were lined with palms to the ceiling and the entire altar was covered with rare blooms and foliage.[52]

The silk dress in Illustration 192 makes quite a contrast to the duchess's elegant gown. It was worn in West Liberty, Iowa, in September 1896. The real allure and beauty of this dress was its simplicity and its yards of very soft, almost sheer white silk material. The back of the skirt was very full, but its true charm could only be seen when the dress was worn and in motion. A sheer chiffon capelet, deeply gathered, was worn over the huge silk sleeves and back; the chiffon was used again as a stand-up ruching above the high stiffened silk collar, also at the elbows, giving a finish to the sleeves. A chiffon flower ornamented the neckline.

Simple in style, this gown came from a small town in the Midwest; it was probably made by the bride or her seamstress. The skirt was simply gathered in two parts, very full on a tiny waistband, giving full play to the beautiful silk. A very heavy petticoat of sized muslin was worn with it; this had a seventeen-inch-deep lined hem of starched linen and four inches of silk. It was finished with a quarter-inch band of velvet at the edge, a perfect undergarment over which the silk could flow. The young woman who wore this dress had a waist measurement of nineteen inches and a bust of twenty-six inches.

The nineteenth century did not have the abundance of printed material we see today. When a monthly fashion magazine arrived, articles concerning the current weddings were avidly read. The fashion writers fed their readers the most minute details about the clothes worn, first describing the bride's complete outfit, then the bridesmaids', the bride's and groom's mothers', and in many instances a complete rundown of the wedding guests' outfits. One account listed the costumes of at least thirty distinguished lady guests at a wedding. Usually the customs, the receptions, and settings were described also.

By early 1896, sleeves had ballooned out to the fullest proportions they would reach. The huge sleeve (with its stiffening and lining) dominated the entire costume, overwhelming the top of the hourglass shape (see Ill. 194).

Illustration 195 is a fine example of the style of gown at the end of the century (1898). The gown of ivory silk satin had a raised rib and used hand-made Honiton bobbin lace.

Fashion seekers quickly tire of any extreme style. Full sleeves disappeared in the summer months of 1896. They began to sag from the shoulder, and a tart little epaulette crowned the shoulder. The bosom soon gained emphasis and fullness, a prelude to our modern-day fascination with this portion of female anatomy.

In a society wedding in December 1897, the bride's veil was worn in a new style fashionable in the East. Falling from beneath a coronet of white satin sewn with brilliants, it enveloped the bride with its light drapery. The photograph in Illustration 198 shows the bride's gown of white duchesse satin; the bodice was cut low off the shoulders, finished with a triple ruffle of magnificent old point d' Alençon lace inherited from her grandmother. Sprays of orange blossoms were worn on the shoulders, one of which was adorned with a circular pin of diamonds. She carried a large bouquet of bride roses.[53]

Again we show a simple gown in cream-colored, lightweight silk twill (Ill. 199); it had no lace, no beads, no pearls, or braids. Its beauty lay in the fine detailing, the ornamentation of self-material in deeply gathered ruching on skirt and sleeves, and in the lustrous silk. The skirt was full, the gores in the back cut on the bias; there was a twelve-inch placket opening in the skirt and a graceful train. The hem was weighted with hem lining and white velvet. There were sixteen hooks and eyes at the front closing, and a double ribbon bow at center waist. Five half-inch tucks formed the high collar. This gown was worn by a Pennsylvania bride from Camp Hill at her April 1899 wedding; it was made by a seamstress in Elizabethtown, Pennsylvania.

As the century ended, ornate, rich gowns were widespread. Although the Victorian ideal and sense of modesty lingered, a new feeling—a genuine sense of freedom—pervaded the female world. In fact, as women emerged from a structured domestic life, their lives were changing dramatically.

Fashion reflected the independence women were experiencing. In the 1890s, the concept of Haute Couture was becoming a must for fashionable women.

Part III

Twentieth Century

10

New Century, New Look (1900-1915)

One way to accept a trendy new style is to consider the past style outmoded or old-fashioned. Although the woman of 1900 was not yet "liberated," in mind and spirit she saw a different world where she could throw off past suppressions. Bustles and bows, long trains and balloon sleeves were things of the past.

Transition to a new look in the twentieth century took the usual, gradual development. Modern streamlining began with gentle, fluid lines before the austere, boxlike shapes became fashionable. The early 1900s corset was a straight-front undergarment that gave a new look of curves to the woman's body (see Ill. 206 in this chapter). Cut lower down, it dropped the bustline, making it appear full. Suspenders attached to the bottom of the corset kept it taut and

straight; but as the waist was small, the hips, sides, and back swelled out, producing a distinct "S" curve to a woman's shape. Freedom in dress came a little later; for example, when a woman discovered that it was impossible to drive an automobile in a tight corset, she longed to discard it altogether.

For this new woman there were still Victorian pressures: a proper wedding was essential. A "perfectly appointed" wedding had complex requirements, ruled by the dictates of etiquette. One bride from Austin, Texas, had such a wedding in May 1901. Her portrait in the gown she wore (Ill. 201) shows a superb creation of pale blue embroidered crêpe de chine, trimmed with duchesse lace. Carrying a shower of white roses, she was wholly enveloped in a bridal veil of white

ILLUSTRATION 201.

ILLUSTRATION 202.

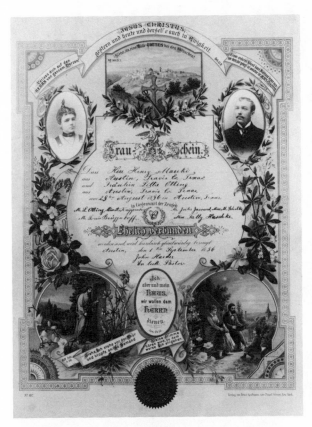

ILLUSTRATION 203. *The marriage certificate of Fraulein Lillie Otting and Herr Henry Maerki, August 29, 1896.*

ILLUSTRATION 204.

tulle, but was photographed without the veil or flowers. Today her large brocade-and-gold wedding album has been preserved. Filled with photographs (see Ill. 202), pressed flowers, and newspaper accounts, it also contains swatches of material of the complete trousseau and wedding dress. Her marriage certificate—large, colorful, and ornately illustrated with flowers—has also been preserved.

Many marriage certificates from the mid-nineteenth century to the 1920s were huge, ornate, beautiful works of art that were framed and saved. The average size of these certificates is eighteen by thirteen inches; the outside measurement, twenty-two by seventeen inches. Many libraries have stored these fine documents, along with other family records.

One certificate in German is in full color, with soft-colored borders and portraits of the bridal couple. The groom was from Switzerland, but they were married in Austin, Texas, in 1896. (For a photo of the bride and groom, see Ill. 193, Chapter 9.) Some certificates include a photograph of the officiating clergyman. One in the author's family, dated 1887, measures fourteen by eighteen inches, unframed. Although not in color, it contains fine steel engravings, photographs of the bride, groom, and pastor.

It was fashionable at this time to have the bridal photograph without flowers or veil, and one can easily see why by looking at the magazine cover in Illustration 205. Here, a young bride is so surrounded by voluminous tulle that she has to compete with overornamentation of the setting,

THE LADIES' HOME JOURNAL

NOVEMBER
1900

TEN
CENTS

THE CURTIS PUBLISHING COMPANY PHILADELPHIA

ILLUSTRATION 205.

ILLUSTRATION 206.

whether church, chapel, or home. It is hard to find the bride herself among so much splendor.

The high dog collar was definitely in vogue in 1900. In 1942, the American couturier Mainbocher revived the style when he designed Mrs. John C. Wilson's pearls in a three-string necklace. But in the Gay Nineties, when Lillian Russell and Maxine Elliott were popular beauties, wealthy women had dog collars of diamonds and pearls fitted to plaster replicas of their own throats. The fashion was started by the most famous bride of the 1890s, Consuelo Vanderbilt. (For a description of her elegant wedding, see Chapter 9.) Consuelo had a long neck, described as "swanlike." She wore a wide, tight collar of jewels—diamonds and pearls. The fashion was borrowed from lap dogs, which were in great vogue at the time.[54]

In the first dozen years of the twentieth century, the high neckline—as high as two or two and a half inches—continued to flourish. The dog collar was often worn with a gown's lowered neckline to achieve a high, elongated look (see Ill. 223).

On April 22, 1903, a young career woman was married in a Philadelphia home on North Fifty-second Street. Although hers was not a church wedding, she was attended by a matron of honor, a bridesmaid, two flower girls, and she had an organist. Her lovely gown, satin slip, corset-cover, petticoat, and shoes have all been preserved (see Ill. 206). The dress was embroidered net, reembroidered with pearls and beads. Pearl medallions were fastened at the corners of the yoke and center front waistline. Ribbon was threaded through the ornate braid above the deep full net ruffle.

Soft white cotton fabrics were favored by women who had less formal or home weddings.

ILLUSTRATION 207. *This is a wedding portrait of a couple married in Tucson, Arizona, in May 1901. The bride's dress was a two-piece ivory satin. The bodice had a yoke of shirred organza. The sleeves were fitted, with an overpiece of pleated organza, giving a puffed effect below the elbow. The trained skirt had a dust ruffle and an edging of velvet corduroy under the hem.*

ILLUSTRATION 208. *This dress, designed with artistic skill, used an embroidered motif of the lily very effectively. The long, padded train was heavily embroidered with silk floss in a large pattern of lilies and leaves. The lily motif was repeated on the bodice. The V-neck and sleeves were edged with bugle beads, which were also interspersed in the lily pattern in train and bodice. Brussels lace bordered the Empire waistline and formed part of the sleeves. A braided satin thread outlined the pattern and connecting latticework.*

ILLUSTRATION 209. *This dress was made by the bride for a summer wedding in 1903 at her parents' home in Brooklyn.*

ILLUSTRATION 210. *A bride praying (1905).*

Organdy, cotton lawn, embroidered muslins, and dotted swiss were used, as were sheer linen, lawn, and silk mull. These lightweight materials could be finely tucked and augmented with inserts of lace edgings, ribbons, and eyelets. The resulting dresses epitomized daintiness and delicacy.

Whatever the fabric, it could be converted into many eye-pleasing surfaces or textures. Some dresses may have taken a full year to make because of exquisite hand-stitched work on sheer materials, laces, and eyelets. Dresses were made with careful detail from 1900–1910 to give an impression of flowing motion; skirts rippled over hips and undulated around the feet. They were graceful, elegant, and comfortable.

Howard Chandler Christy's drawing of a bride and groom for a magazine cover, March 1905, very graphically shows the fashionable "S" curve of the day (see Ill. 116, Chapter 7). This illustration was marketed in 1905 for sale as a poster, "The Famous Christy Girl as a Bride."

One wedding in November 1906 in Houston, Texas, was surrounded by a great deal of planning and activity. A young Texas beauty, prominent in Jewish society, married a respected Philadelphian of the clothing firm of M. Snellenburg & Company. The wedding took place on the bride's twenty-first birthday in her grandmother's splendid home.

The bride descended the stairway into the large

ILLUSTRATION 211. *This eighteen-year-old, married in 1907, looks like a Gibson Girl in her bridal outfit.*

hall, which had been transformed into a rose arbor. Her wedding gown was a magnificent Empire style, fashioned of heavy white satin, hand-embroidered in white and silver with point appliqué trimming. It was hemstitched by hand. She wore a fine diamond brooch, a gift from the groom, as well as a collar studded with dia-monds, from her parents, and a string of pearls. Her long, sweeping veil was of tulle. The shower bridal bouquet was of orchids and lilies of the valley tied with broad satin ribbons, and she carried an ivory prayer book with gold monogram.

Each room was extensively decorated with deli-cate foliage, vines, a profusion of American

ILLUSTRATION 212. *"Dressing the Bride"* (1907).

Beauty roses, chrysanthemums, and carnations. The society column of the *Houston Chronicle,* which described the wedding, noted every detail, as well as the orchestra, the gowns of out-of-town guests, and also a list of the invited guests. The following accessories accompanied the bride's gown: a small white wreath attached to the veil with orange blossoms, long white kid gloves, a small Bible, a lace holder for flowers, and long white silk stockings with a floral and vine design

in silver thread embroidery, white satin, and beads.

The same year (1906) also marked the wedding of Alice Roosevelt Longworth ("Princess Alice"), who lived in the White House.

In Illustration 212, a 1907 bride is assisted into her finery. Again, the woman of the early 1900s was guided by what was "proper" and usually followed rules and regulations rigidly. In fact, it was so important to the young bride to

ILLUSTRATION 213.
A wedding dress of 1908.

ILLUSTRATION 214. *A nineteen-inch German bisque doll by Simon Halbig wears an antique "Irish crochet" lace wedding dress. It was fashioned by the owner, who was inspired by the dress worn by her own grandmother on her wedding day in June 1913. The dress has seed pearls and a satin sash. The headpiece is of antique silk tulle with antique wax flowers. The gloves are white kid. The bride doll carries a bouquet of the same wax flowers and knotted antique ribbon.*

prove she was married that she carried the license along with her on her honeymoon. There were even embroidered cases for carrying the marriage certificate in the bride's trunk in travels across the country.

Many dresses of 1908–1910 were completely covered with eyelet, embroidered bands, and lace—at the time considered things of genuine beauty.

Country Weddings

Country weddings were filled with every bit as much planning, activity, and joyous celebration as city society weddings; tradition and propriety were just as strong. Handed-down customs gave each new bride the feeling of being among her own.

Country weddings were quite informal. We can imagine the young woman and her mother buying a smooth length of material from a new bolt at the store and spending many happy hours making her new dress for the special day. If all the old traditions were followed, celebrations could go on for days, with music, dancing, and an abundance of food. Or, like a summer wedding in Palatine, Illinois (a suburb of Chicago), in 1911, it could be held in the backyard, where an arch was built and decorated with wildflowers from the countryside. The dress at that wedding, made in Chicago, cost $50.

After 1910, softer, finer cottons were available. The popular set-in sleeves had cluny lace insertions alternating with sheer cotton embroidered voile, as did the skirt. The neckline to the base of the throat was perfect for wearing the fashionable dog collar of pearl strands. A single large rose tucked under hair arranged in a knot provided all that was needed for the outdoor head dressing. The psyche knot was a very popular way of arranging the hair from 1906–12. Makeup was considered too worldly and cheap by the middle class, and so very little, if any, was worn.

The 1912 gown in Illustration 217 is more sophisticated. Like contemporary clothing, it forecasts a decided change in female appearance. Features that were emphasized—bust and hips and a very small waistline—were downplayed in a more masculine line. Flat over the hips and bust,

ILLUSTRATION 215. *This postcard shows a Hun wedding party in Lykens, Pennsylvania.*

ILLUSTRATION 216. *A 1910 wedding party gathers around a bridal table.*

ILLUSTRATION 217.

ILLUSTRATION 218. *This 1914 wedding dress was of machine-made needle lace, point d'Alencon; the cape, cut on the bias, was pleated at the two top corners, sewn to lingerie pins, and then attached. Current style decreed that the woman could swath her hips in gleaming white satin, for many dress patterns of this period emphasized the hips. Capes were also highly popular.*

ILLUSTRATION 219. *In a May 1914 dress pattern, a girdle yoke was used to accentuate the straight, waistless side lines.*

ILLUSTRATION 220. *This 1915 bride preferred the traditional pose for the photographer.*

this gown used metallic threads and beads in a sunburst design on the upper bodice. From the Empire waistline, a panel of satin tassels and beads hung down in the center front, obliterating the natural waistline. The back, graceful and elegant, emphasized the tunic design as the metallic beadwork skimmed over the hips. This gown has a sleek and streamlined appearance.

To say that the new century brought a new look is an understatement. The dress of 1914, loose and nonclinging, stands in bold contrast to the corseted, disciplined look of 1900 and earlier.

Paris still reigned supreme in dictating fashions in the years before World War I. Fashion magazines talked about the "Paris Season," and columns describing "What to Wear and When to Wear It" were commonplace, as were charts to help one dress correctly. Paris said everything should be in one piece—skirts, blouses, and wraps. What Paris said was "as the laws of the Medes and Persians to the New York Mondaine."[55] When Paris obliterated the waistline from new fashions, focusing on the line from the shoulder to the edge of a garment only and treating the body as a unit, America obeyed.

11

The Veil and Headdress

In our historical look at the wedding dress, we should not ignore the veil and headpiece; they are part of the complete wedding costume. Many fascinating customs surround them, and a great deal of importance was put on the veil.

The wedding veil did not appear in America until the Empire period, c. 1800. It was not worn at all during the 1700s. Brides of the eighteenth century wore devices for protecting an ornate headdress. One of these coverings was the calash, usually made of silk shirred on strong lengths of rattan or whalebone two or three inches apart and drawn in at the neck by a cape. The calash could extend and fold back like the top or hood of an old-fashioned chaise or calash—from which it received its name. It could be drawn out over the face with ribbons, and then be pushed flatly to the back of the head.

When were veils first worn? Early journals and books give accounts of the earliest wedding veil, made for a wedding dress worn by a Charleston, South Carolina, bride who married at nineteen. Her portrait was painted by the artist Malbone, who was in Charleston in the year 1800. The portrait shows a tulle wedding veil and a splendid tiara of pearls sent to her from England by her godmother as a wedding gift.

Other references to veils date from old illustrations and books. In a little book of crude rhymes entitled *The Courtship and Marriage of Jerry and Kitty,* published in London in 1814, one bride wore over her hair and face a bridal veil that hung to the hem of her gown. In another story, found in *The Dandy's Wedding* (London, 1823), the bride wore a veil hanging from a comb over her face. The accompanying verse reads:

ILLUSTRATION 221. *This veil is arranged in an elaborate hairstyle of 1832 (from a French fashion plate.)*

ILLUSTRATION 222. *These artistically arranged hairstyles and veils are from an 1872 fashion plate.*

ILLUSTRATION 223. *This white velvet dog collar (also called a choker) was worn in 1971.*

The handsome veil of Mechlin lace
  A sister's love bestows.
It adds new beauties to her face
  Which now with pleasure glows.
Friends, brothers, sisters, cousins, meet
  To attend the happy bride:
And Queer's joy is all complete,
  The nuptial knot is tied.[56]

To the Victorian bride, wearing the veil was a symbol of pride. White symbolized purity, and the veil confirmed for all to see that she was virgin.

In an 1896 *Harper's Bazar* (see Ill. 224), the magazine described the coiffure as simple and youthful. The hair was slightly waved, raised loosely to the crown in back, the front taken back

ILLUSTRATION 224.

ILLUSTRATION 225. *A 1910 bridal portrait.*

in a low pompadour. At the back the hair was divided into two strands, twined around each other for half their lengths, then formed into a soft figure-eight knot. Tiny sprays of orange and myrtle were added. The veil was brought together a yard from the upper end and fastened to the hair, with the short end falling over the face; the corners of this end were round. The folds were caught lightly with small veil clasps.

In the years when the pompadour became chic, for a Gibson Girl image, bridal veils were given a back seat, resting on the back of the head.

Called a wreath in the nineteenth century, the headpiece has had many different shapes and names. Shaped like a royal crown, it was called a tiara. It has been shaped into a Juliette cap, a

coronet, a circlet, a diadem, and a bandeau. In 1919, a cap veil of shadow lace was called a boudoir cap; the bride was virtually enveloped in the filmy material of a veil, so the headpiece had to be substantial.

Bonnets have been popular in many periods. A becoming Victorian-style bonnet of "heavenly blue" velveteen was worn by a Texas bride in 1948. The bonnet was shirred and peaked in center front, corded around the edge, and tied under the chin, with the bow on the left side. Several layers of blue tulle veiling formed the crown and fell around the shoulders to the waist. The bride's dress was also of blue velveteen (see Chapter 15). The entire trousseau was saved, including dress, bonnet, bridesmaids' dresses, bride's going-away

ILLUSTRATIONS 226 & 227.
Two cap-style veils of 1914.

ILLUSTRATION 228.

suit, cocktail dress, and pictures.

The 1960s and the 1970s brought freedom from convention and tradition. Brides wore simple flower clusters, ribbons in attractive hairdos, or the very alluring picture hat.

Compare today's prices to an offer in a Sears Roebuck catalogue c. 1901–1902. A bridal wreath, described as "of extra quality" cost 85¢.

ILLUSTRATION 229. *A midsummer wedding in 1979, with a college chapel setting, is pictured here. The bride wore real flowers, arranged in coronet fashion by her hairdresser. In the wreath were five stephanotis flowers and baby's breath clusters. Her bouquet was of English ivy, spider plant, natal plum, stephanotis, and dieffenbachia.*

It was made of wax orange blossoms; if a brooch and bouquet were included, it cost $1.65.

Throughout American history, the veil (and more specifically, the headdress) took innumer-able forms, as did the wedding dress itself. New styles, new trends, and a great deal of creative designing entered into the fashioning of the crowning point of the entire costume.

12

Underclothing

Despite our focus on the bride's dress, we should not ignore the undergarments beneath those shapely gowns! Our minds are no longer laced by the Victorian ideals that whispered about underclothing and set taboos. Many a bride in the nineteenth and twentieth centuries considered underclothes "unmentionables." Today those taboos have nearly vanished.

Undergarments were crucial in forming a beautiful outer design. Just as in architecture the foundation of a building determines the superstructure, so it does on the human figure as well. Corsets, farthingales, hoopskirts, girdles, bustles, and bust forms were prominent items of underwear. In the sixteenth and seventeenth centuries, European culture could produce a very complicated farthingale, in hoopskirt form, ex-

tending out from the body in the shape of a wheel constructed from hoops of wire, wood, or whalebone; the skirt fell to the ground at the extended rim of this structure. Sometimes the farthingale was made of felt, horsehair, or later, of metal. With these as foundations under the rich brocades of the gowns, women were luxuriously dressed, but inconvenience was the rule of the day.

In the undeveloped new land of America, it was nearly impossible to amass the rich clothing of prevailing European styles. If outer clothing had to be simpler in fabric and style, underclothing was even more so. The farthingale, when worn at all in the colonies, was a plain bolster roll of cloth with a soft filling. It rested just below the waist, and was often called a "bum roll"; the skirt

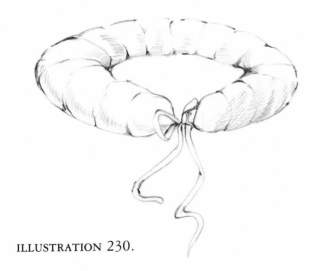

ILLUSTRATION 230.

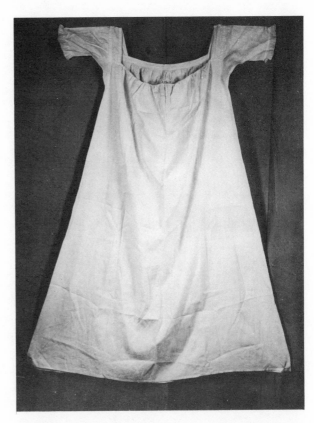

ILLUSTRATION 231. *This chemise of linen, worn in 1838, had puffed sleeves, with a one-and-a-half-inch "handkerchief" linen ruffle at the sleeve edge. The wide neckline was reinforced at the corners and a linen drawstring tied at the front edge. The garment had fine hemstitching.*

flared out over it (see Ill. 230). Paniers, those basketlike projections worn under each side of the skirt in the eighteenth century, were simply made of reeds or whalebone. Imported ones were more elaborate. Pioneer women and most country women in the eighteenth and early nineteenth century wore a simple linen chemise, as the one shown in Illustration 231.

In the mid-nineteenth century there was increasing interest in voluminous skirts. Multiple layers of petticoats, coupled with dresses with tiers of flounces, became too cumbersome. The cage crinoline was designed to remedy this. The first innovation was a deep facing of crinoline, a stiff wool and horsehair petticoat. Since it was almost as heavy as the multiple starched petticoats, the cage crinoline, a petticoat of whalebone or watch-spring hoops held together with broad tapes, was invented in 1856. Women of all ages and classes snatched it up. It freed them of the cumbersome weight, yet held skirts out for yards (see Ills. 232 and 233).

These new crinolines were scientifically designed, for technology in America was now sufficiently advanced that the manufacturers were able to supply flexible steel hoops that could either form a separate garment hung by tapes from the waist, or be sewn into a petticoat.[57] The fad became fashion, and women everywhere wanted it—*had* to have it. Fairly inexpensive and lightweight, it could swing and be in a constant state of motion; but it needed plenty of room!

The hoopskirt crinoline became dome-shaped about 1858–59; in the early 1860s it reached its most expansive proportions. Changing shape as it flattened in front, it led the way to the bustle around 1869.

The bustle's shape evolved from one form to another as the whim of fashion demanded. There was a small wire crinoline in 1870; also a combination of a small panier and crinoline or crinolette. In 1870, the "tilter" appeared; it was a

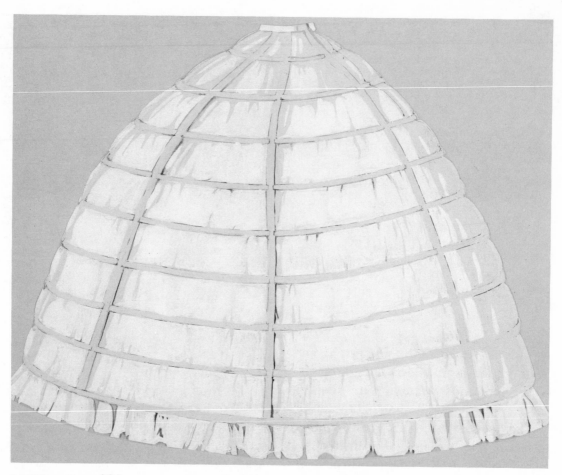

ILLUSTRATION 232.

bustle resembling the tournure,* except that the shirring containing the springs was in a separate piece and was adjustable. In 1871, the side of the bustle extended over the hip and above the waist. Then, in 1873, the bustle became narrower and longer. Around 1874, the tournure and the bustle disappeared altogether.

Many brides preferred to make their own lingerie (see Ill. 234). Undergarments were by no means as ornate in the 1890s as they were in years past. The finest French lingerie was handmade and trimmed with small net scallops and narrow Valenciennes lace. Groups of pin tucks might alternate with the insertion lace.

*A type of French bustle that replaced many petticoats; steel springs passed through shirring across the back, secured in front by strings.

The corset fashioned at the beginning of the twentieth century was very distinctive. At first, the design retained an hourglass shape, as shown in Illustration 235. The new, straight-front corset appeared in the fall of 1901. This item truly distorted the natural form of the body, thrusting the upper front of the body forward, and the lower part of the body back, to make a distinct "S" curve. Women who wore this item felt off-balance.

In the spring of 1903, women could buy corsets made of fine French coutil (a sturdy fabric constructed of a compactly woven herringbone twill, in drab or white, sateen or batiste); Valenciennes lace with two side steels and four bone strips; Imperial drill (a strong twilled cotton fabric) with satin ribbons; and sublime jean, trimmed at the top with satin ribbon and bow-

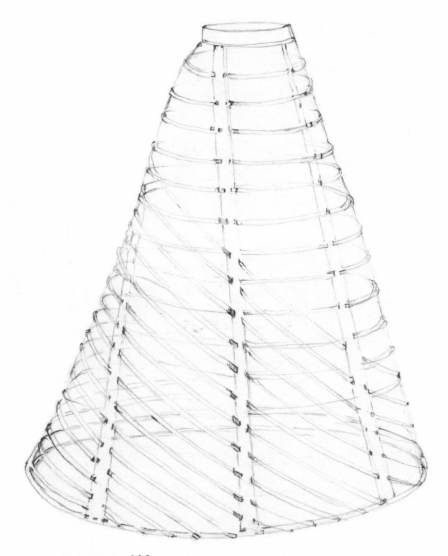

ILLUSTRATION 233.

knot finish, with a dip bust and long skirt, low back, and hose tabs at the lower front point.[58] In this period, "jean" was a twilled cotton, dyed or bleached, and used for boot and shoe linings, corsets, and other items of clothing.

As seen in Illustration 237, advertisements in womens' fashion magazines often showed the inside of the corset in an attempt to prove its comfort. Yet in spite of the very real discomfort of the corset and bust bodice, these garments added poise and gave a very sophisticated and elegant look. It was called the pigeon-breast look, the dyspepsia front, the kangaroo pouch, among other names. The bust bodice, which had been

worn since its introduction in 1889, has been called a "monobra." Bust pads and girdles, which we think of as modern, were actually sewn into some wedding dresses in the early 1800s, some even earlier.

The mature woman was idealized for this straight-front corset and "S" look. Later, the youthful look came into fashion, but during this period a fashionable woman longed for a full figure. She sought the massive rounded front, and the straight-front corset gave it to her. The look appears plump to our contemporary eye.

Another ploy to create curves was the wire hip pad and bustle (see Ill. 239). Made of highly

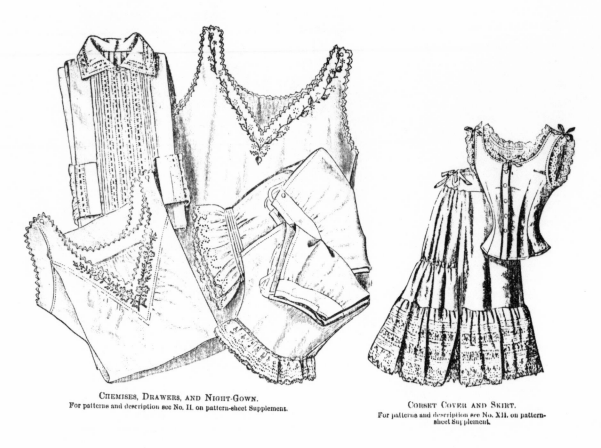

CHEMISES, DRAWERS, AND NIGHT-GOWN.
For patterns and description see No. II. on pattern-sheet Supplement.

CORSET COVER AND SKIRT.
For patterns and description see No. XII. on pattern-sheet Supplement.

ILLUSTRATION 234.

tempered, black enameled woven wire, bustles cost around 19¢. The skirt and waist holder was also an aid in grooming.

Women in the early 1900s gave much attention to each piece of clothing in their trousseaux, sometimes doing extra embroidery and monogramming on certain pieces. Underclothing was no exception. From the fabric closest to the skin, to the accessory that was pure adornment, it was important that everything be special for the bride.

At this time, around 1901, the "dip" became fashionable; the skirt was cut at the waistline, with a decided dip at the center front. This downward tendency showed in the girdle sash and in the fall of the skirt. Designers aimed for a flowing line; a skirt swept closely over the hips, forming broad undulations about the feet.

After the torturous decades of the laced corset, the twentieth century brought a great liberation from that confinement. As the corset disappeared, woman's body was not left unsupported; the talented French couturier Poiret designed a new, light rubber girdle to pull in the hips and stomach. Just as the bustle's shape evolved from one form to another, the girdle has undergone many changes until the present day.

Sixteenth-century European women girded themselves with substantial undergarments for an eye-pleasing outer effect. There was rigid struc-

ILLUSTRATION 235. *An advertisement in May 1900.*

ILLUSTRATION 236. *An advertisement in September 1901.*

ILLUSTRATION 237. *A corset advertisement, February 1900.*

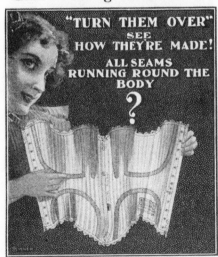

THOMSON'S
"Glove=Fitting" CORSETS

"TURN THEM OVER"
SEE
HOW THEY'RE MADE!

ALL SEAMS
RUNNING ROUND THE
BODY
?

Require no "BREAKING IN" because the **seams** of the corset fit so accurately over the **lines** of the body that you do not realize you have changed the old corset for the new. Prices from **$1** to **$5** per pair.

If your dealer does not sell our corsets, send to us.

Send for Handsome Illustrated Catalogue, MAILED FREE

LANGDON, BATCHELLER & CO.
345 Broadway, - New York City

When You Get Married

Let us furnish your WEDDING INVITATIONS. Send for Samples and Prices. 30 years' experience at the business. C. E. HOUGHTALING, 100 Madison Avenue, ALBANY, N.Y.

ILLUSTRATION 238. *A "monobra," or bust bodice, worn around 1900. The bust bodices worn around the turn of the century were usually boned and sometimes laced in the front and back.*

ILLUSTRATION 239. *An advertisement for wire hip pads and bustles (1902).*

The Parisienne Wire Bustle.

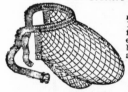

No.18R4876 The Parisienne Woven Wire Bustle, made of highly tempered, black enameled, woven wire. The best shape, which it will always retain.
Price, each.........19c
If by mail, postage extra, 5 cents.

Parisienne Hip Pad and Bustle.

No. 18R4880 The Parisienne Hip Pad and Bustle, made of best tempered, black enameled, woven wire with hip pads of padded cloth. Perfect in shape, and light in weight. Very durable.
Price, each,..40c

If by mail, postage extra, each, 10 cents.

The Duchess Hip Pad and Bustle.

No. 18R4884 The Duchess Woven Wire Hip Pad and Bustle, made of best woven white wire, correct shape, very light and durable, and equal to any sold elsewhere for 75 cents or $1.00.
Price, each...39c

If by mail, postage extra, 11 cents.

The Lenox Glove Fitting Hip Bustle.

No. 18R4886
It rounds out the figure and produces the effect desired in prevailing fashions, extending over the hips very lightly and gracefully. Made of blue black tempered steel and cannot get out of shape, neither can it be detected. Suitable for rainy day skirts.

Price, each 37c
If by mail, postage extra, 10 cents.

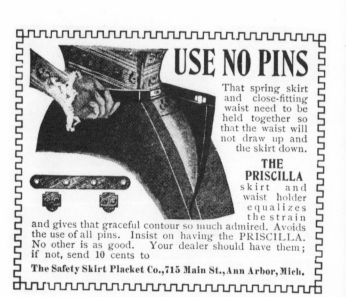

USE NO PINS

That spring skirt and close-fitting waist need to be held together so that the waist will not draw up and the skirt down.

THE PRISCILLA skirt and waist holder equalizes the strain and gives that graceful contour so much admired. Avoids the use of all pins. Insist on having the PRISCILLA. No other is as good. Your dealer should have them; if not, send 10 cents to
The Safety Skirt Placket Co.,715 Main St.,Ann Arbor,Mich.

ILLUSTRATION 240. *Skirt and waist holder.*

ILLUSTRATION 241. *This 1901 bridal dress had a full-pouched bodice, emphasized by a bow of sheer material tacked to the lower center of the yoke and at the waistline. The bow accessory gave a loose, ballooning effect.*

ILLUSTRATION 242. *The blue garter has been popular for nearly a hundred years. The one illustrated here is from 1903. How bridal couples, even today, love the custom of removing the bride's garter!*

ture underneath gowns, intended to present outwardly soft, flowing lines and easy fullness to skirts and smallness to waists.

American and European women always have shown a willingness to bind themselves and to carry steel or whalebone cages underneath showy dress. This has been the fashion until fairly recently.

13

Woman's Emancipation
(1915 - 1930)

In the years from 1915 to 1930, fashion experimented with everything in its sphere, from necklines to skirt lengths. It began to scorn boned corseting and replaced it with sagging waistlines; skirts were hiked up as never before or pulled down in uneven points. Fashion, it seemed, could not let the natural body outline alone. It camouflaged the waistline completely and at times confined the legs and knees in a tube, as in the 1914 peg-top silhouette. Sometimes the whole torso was allowed to droop.

Even so, talented dress designers came up with decidedly fresh approaches to clothing the female figure. Some revealed the figure beautifully; others used artistry in color and color combinations. Still others invented a new shape. The bride of this period was emancipated from the overly constricting clothing of the past. Such freedom was a luxury.

Much was happening in the period from 1914 to 1930. The personalities who influenced America ranged from Lindbergh, Edison, and

ILLUSTRATION 243. *A 1915 Dallas bride wore this pencil-slim blue suit from Neiman-Marcus. It had a long, hip-length jacket with princess line; four gores in the jacket side gave sufficient fullness. Top-stitched in satin thread, it was lined in silk. The skirt was a wraparound, plain, well detailed and tailored, eased onto a quarter-inch waistband of satin.*

ILLUSTRATION 244. *The shoes worn with the suit in Ill. 243 are made of black leather and beige suede.*

ILLUSTRATION 246. *Detail of the dress design and wedding shoes of the gown in Illustration 245.*

ILLUSTRATION 245. *True to the mode of 1915, this nearly shapeless wedding dress artfully emphasizes ornamental detail. It was made of silk chiffon, satin, and lace. Draping was a prominent feature; the lace was caught up and tacked in various places by pearl clusters and tassels, and it hung in peaks in the back. There was a high, stand-up collar in the back.*

ILLUSTRATION 247. *Photograph of a bride in her 1916 wedding dress of sheer paper-weight organza, lined in satin. A decorative wisteria design, hand-embroidered, trailed up the front of the skirt.*

Henry Ford to Frank Lloyd Wright, Aaron Copland, and Picasso. And for women, Susan B. Anthony's influence and cause, carried on today, led to freedom for women. On August 28, 1920, the Nineteenth Amendment to the U.S. Constitution was ratified, giving women the right to vote.

Despite radical changes in the times, wedding dresses were still considered costumes of moderation. Some brides hesitated to wear an innovative style, so most gowns from the time seem very traditional and out-of-date. The dazzling fashions of the 1920s were not generally reflected in bridal dresses. Nonetheless, they managed to be enchanting.

Since many young men were serving in Europe during World War I, weddings sometimes had to be quickly planned for the time when the young man in uniform was home. (Except for nurses and Red Cross workers, few women served during this war, unlike World War II.) But even during wartime there were women who planned sumptuous weddings, importing gowns from Paris and carrying out elaborate receptions. Illustration 248 shows a 1917 Worth gown in silk illusion embroidered with genuine seed pearls in floral motif and trimmed with orange blossoms.

The dress in Illustrations 253 and 254, found in the Arizona Costume Institute, is a genuine work of art in fabric, embroidery, and styling. Made of pineapple fibers in the Philippine Islands (c. 1900), it took twenty women eight months to weave and embroider the cloth. Then, in 1927, Henri Bendel of New York City designed and made the dress, which is pale pink in color. The dress had side paniers, which came back, briefly, at this time. The pink paniered hoop petticoat was wired flat in front and extended at the sides. The deep, graceful bertha collar extended over the arms and dipped in back to the natural waistline. The waistline also dipped in back, as did the hemline. As a result of this cut in designing, the dress was cocktail length in front, and reached almost to the floor in the back. There is a second bodice to this costume, styled in an earlier period, possibly made when the fabric was embroidered. A voluminous tulle veil with a half-inch border of silver lamé was worn with the beautiful gown.

ILLUSTRATION 248.

WOMAN'S WORLD

JUNE · 1929   *"June Wedding Belles"*   15 CENTS A COPY

MARRIAGE—*SIX INTERESTING MESSAGES FROM OTHER DAYS*

Fiction · Fashions · Health and Beauty · Needlework · Sewing · Child Care
Homemaking · Gardening · Cookery · Verse · And Subscribers' Contributions

CHILDREN'S FEATURE, "WHY THE SUN HURRIED" *By Richard Kilroy*

ILLUSTRATION 249. *Magazine cover illustration,* Woman's World, *June 1929.*

ILLUSTRATION 250. *This 1928 gown was of cream soft-ribbed, satin-backed silk, lightly watered. Combined with cream Alencon-type lace, it had two lace flounces mounted on a short chiffon underskirt. A full, open-fronted silk overskirt was trained and gathered onto the low waistline, curving from center front. There are tape-weights around the back of the train. The gown had long lace sleeves.*

ILLUSTRATION 251. *This dress style turns up in nearly every museum's costume collection. Of light-weight satin, lace, and chiffon, it was worn at a 1925 wedding in Easton, Pennsylvania. It had a floating satin panel in front, from the wide bateau neckline to the waist. Originally there was a free-floating panel train (often referred to as a "fish-tail" train) in back. Attached by snaps to the back neckline, it could be removed to convert the dress into a ball gown.*

ILLUSTRATION 253.

ILLUSTRATION 252. *In Houston, Texas, a bride wore a dress very similar in style to that in Ill. 251, with the very same belt treatment of pearls and beads at the lowered waistline. Also of satin, it had a gathered chiffon neckline and seven appliqués, seven inches across, of the gathered chiffon, centered with a pearl pin in high relief. Included in this bride's trousseau is an ecru corset with lace, a short slip of silk, wide-leg silk "step-ins," a petticoat with lace, and a silk nightgown.*

ILLUSTRATION 254.

ILLUSTRATION 255.

ILLUSTRATION 256. *This Paris-made wedding dress for an Austin bride (1927)*
was in a traditional style.

ILLUSTRATION 257. *An Atlanta doctor's daughter (1928) wore a satin dress with the year's short skirt and a satin "handkerchief point" at the hip, a typical fashion touch of the 1920s.*

In Illustration 255, the sleeveless, ecru georgette gown of a June 1925 bride was all but hidden by the swathing veil and sizable bouquet. The georgette of the dress was worn over an attached satin slip. It was a low-waisted style; the top of the bodice, waistline, and skirt were heavily decorated with white and clear beads, pearls, and chenille, in a floral design. The top and hem of the slip were decorated with a metallic lace trim. The bride wore the brow-hugging headpiece of the current season.

The skirts of 1926 and 1927 were the shortest of the decade—just below the knee. Although many mothers raised eyebrows and gasped in dis-

ILLUSTRATION 258. *This ivory silk chiffon wedding dress was worn in 1927. Sleeveless, with a dropped waist, its overskirt is in separate panels. The waistband and lower edges of the bodice and skirt are edged with crystal beads, metallic yarn, and rhinestones in stylized floral patterns.*

approval, the days of freedom—even for the bride—were here. Only those who insisted on tradition continued to wear gowns to the floor.

The examples shown in this chapter give an overview of the shape of dress and freedom of movement women now had. It was a clear departure from the skirt that reached the floor and the dress that hugged the shapely body. Here was quite a nondescript look; it had great influence on future fashion.

14

The Elite of Us and the Rest of Us

Weddings, whether filled with all the accoutrements of lavish decor, clothing, and accessories, or simply a gathering of man, woman, and a few friends, are historical events. Ceremonies in different areas of the country can be markedly dissimilar.

One Atlanta bride, married in 1942, wore a champagne-colored satin peau gown with family heirloom lace (see Ill. 259). Using several period styles, her gown was reminiscent of the 1860s, with its hoop and "balmoral" petticoat. One of Atlanta's fine stores at that time, Rich's Bridal Shop, obligingly altered this gown to the young lady's specifications, adding the family rosepoint lace. The rosepoint over silk tulle was used at yoke and hem; the hooped overskirt was pleated and drawn up on each side front to form scallops

decorated with flower clusters. The skirt was twelve-gored with a cathedral train. Four other members of the bride's family wore this beautiful gown in later years.

In June of the same year (1942), the bride in Illustration 260 chose a very simple marquisette dress of the prevailing style of the forties. Because it was wartime, scant yardage was used in softly flowing lines, yet the back of the gown trailed off into a long train. Fabric daisies outlined the sweetheart neckline, and the back closed with nineteen covered buttons. There are as many diverse kinds of dresses as there are brides to pick them. In this marriage (Ill. 260), the groom was an ordained minister and the bride had no desire to be ostentatious. Thrilled with her chosen partner and the life they were embarking on together,

ILLUSTRATION 259.

ILLUSTRATION 260.

ion plate, *Godey's Lady's Book* portrayed a bride's dress using lace. It is interesting to note that this Philadelphia fashion magazine prided itself in being singularly American. It explained itself as "Paris Fashions 'Americanized.'"

The beautiful handmade laces were genuine art, examples of a truly creative industry. Handmade lace was so expensive that it was often removed and sewn onto one gown after another, working its way through numerous generations. "Heirloom" lace, treasured in a family for years, had an elegance that even the least wealthy could wear and enjoy. Certainly the growing, rural, partially undeveloped country of nineteenth century America was the last place to house rich laces. But even those who felt the pinch of finances influenced fashion.

One can only imagine how many weddings have taken place in areas where circumstances demand meager means. (Even today America has areas of wilderness, where obedience to social rules is meaningless; where elegant clothing would not only be impossible but unreasonable.) In a remote region, the fundamentals might be a simple recitation of a form and a bridal dress of new cotton or calico with a fresh apron (see Ill. 261).

One young woman who longed for an elaborate wedding in 1914 had limited resources and had to plan carefully and do her own sewing to have the kind of dress she wanted (see Ill. 262). With only $25, fulfillment of the dream seemed like an impossibility. After searching, she found some soft, ivory-colored silk with a satiny sheen, forty inches wide, only $1.69 a yard. Princess lace was the only trimming she used, with knotted rosettes of the satin where the folds of silk crossed in the front, and in the back where the train began. The exact cost was:

she was unconcerned with having an elegant gown and chose the marquisette.

Many factors affect the choice of wedding dress—the economy of the country, geographical location, financial circumstance, parental wishes, military affiliation, love of formality and display. Some young women, wrapped up in the drama of a wedding, feel compelled to be conspicuous. American wedding dresses of the early nineteenth century seem largely simple and unadorned. Not many used the fine handmade laces of the low countries of Europe or of Germany, France, Italy, and Great Britain, to name a few. Some very elite American girls wore wedding dresses with special laces imported from a favorite source abroad, but most did without such luxuries. In an 1840 fash-

ILLUSTRATION 261. *A wedding in the back woods of Tennessee.*

6 yards of Silk, at	$10.14
Lace.	3.00
India Silk for waist lining	.75
Making	9.00
Total	$22.89

For the veil she bought three yards of tulle (two-yard width) at $1.25 a yard, with a triple string of pearl beads to band it at the back. A cluster of ribbon rosebuds fastened it above the ear and a tulle rosette finished it on the right. The veil framed the face with a cap effect. Gloves and slippers were other accessories, but by careful purchasing the bride was able to keep within the limitation of her pocketbook. The following figures give the prices:

3 yards of tulle	$3.75
Pearl band.	1.00
Roses.	.25
Long kid gloves.	1.85
Satin slippers.	2.25
White silk stockings	.89
Total	9.99

The Bride Whose Gown Cost $22.89

ILLUSTRATION 262.

ILLUSTRATION 263.

Her flowers were a gift from the groom. The bouquet was simple, consisting of bridal roses and white sweet peas, to harmonize with the costume. She wore a soft, lingerie princesse slip under the wedding dress, saving the expense of a silk underdress. The complete cost of the gown and all its details was $32.88. The wedding dress did double duty when it was worn at the wedding of the bride's maid of honor.

There are other happy ways of arriving at a satisfying nuptial pageant despite limited funds. A clever bride in 1970 selected an inexpensive bridesmaid's dress to wear as her wedding gown (see Ill. 263). It was particularly charming in an out-of-doors setting. The gown, made of ivory linen and banded in pink grosgrain ribbon, was embroidered in shades of pink and green. She carried a bouquet of pink orchids, roses, and carnations.

On the other end of the spectrum, one elegant lady lingers in memory for many of us. Grace Kelly, Philadelphia girl and Hollywood star, became Grace, Princess of Monaco, in April 1956, when she married Prince Rainier III. An account of the splendor that accompanied the event would be a long narration of unmatched scenes—from castle turrets to harbor lights. Hers was a Cinderella wedding, enjoyed by people around the world.

Two wedding gowns were designed for the radiant bride for two festive days; they were created by Hollywood designer Helen Rose of MGM. At an eleven o'clock civil ceremony the first day, the bride wore a costume made of hand-run Alençon lace of blush tan, hand-embroidered on ashes-of-roses silk taffeta to give a three-dimensional brocaded effect. It had a bell-shaped skirt fourteen inches from the ground and a lace

ILLUSTRATION 264.

jacket with lace-covered buttons.

The formal gown for the religious ceremony, made of 450 yards of the finest materials, has been described as the "most lavish ever worn by a bride" (see Ill. 264). In a regal style along Renaissance lines the pale ivory gown and veil took up twenty-five yards of peau de soie, twenty-five yards of silk taffeta, one hundred yards of silk net, and three hundred yards of Valenciennes lace. Thousands of pearls decorated the veil, which was of silk illusion net. The bride wore three petticoats of crêpe and taffeta. Both gowns were made at MGM. No price tag could ever be attached to either work of art.

Newspapers in cities throughout the world carried feature articles about the star bride. Philadelphia, in particular, reveled in proud tales of its beloved princess. Many were tempted to imitate these superb gowns of the Princess of Monaco, including the famous doll maker Martha D. Thompson, who sculpted portrait dolls of the bridal couple in fine porcelain.

We are also reminded of the spectacular wedding in Great Britain in July 1981, which united HRH Prince Charles with Lady Diana Spencer. The bridal dress was universally acclaimed as one of fashion's best creations. Americans were fascinated with it, and many copied the style. And again, dolls depicting the royal couple in bridal dress were made.

15

Some Hollywood-inspired Fashions . . . and Others; Wartime Influences (1930s and 1940s)

The 1930s brought a return to graceful, soft fashions. The excesses of the shapeless form, the short skirt, bobbed hair, and cascades of glittering beads met increasing resistance.

The distnctive style of the late 1920s eased into the 1930s, with its own characteristic look. The dresses with uneven hems in points and enveloping caps with yards and yards of lace veiling echoed the previous years. Large bouquets with cascading ribbons indicated what brides would carry in the next decade. The wedding bouquet became almost too much of an armful!

Most brides still wanted rules of tradition. A gown pattern in the April 26, 1930, issue of *Vogue* was described as formal enough for a ceremony at a cathedral altar, or, without the train, less formal. The satin gown had long sleeves and a court train. *Vogue* described its new pattern as having a "very new, very interesting" cowl neckline, crossed hip yoke, and even skirt length. The back décolletage could be high or low, as desired, and the sleeves, pointed at the wrists, could be omitted. In the illustration, the bridal bouquet was of calla lilies. That particular flower gained such popularity that it was an exclusive favorite, *the* accepted formal bridal flower.

A strange but brief fad emerged around 1933. It was the wearing of black satin wedding dresses with a bridal bouquet of white or yellow calla lilies. This fad did not go unnoticed. The Sunday *Atlanta Journal* magazine of November 26, 1933, presented a photograph of a wedding group where all five women were dressed in black. Having captured the wedding group at a recent fash-

ILLUSTRATION 265. *This gown in the fashionable style of 1933 is two-piece and made of white machine-made lace. Above the long sleeves are two cape flounces at the shoulder. The gown has a long, sleeveless underdress with tiered overskirt. There is an Art Deco rhinestone clasp on the belt.*

ion show in New York, it described the bride and bridesmaids, dressed in deep black, and the bride, who carried white lilies. In the article that followed, black wedding gowns were declared taboo. It said that Atlanta women, past and present, deplored the new style of mourning color for weddings, and they preferred that brides wear white or pastel satin gowns complete with lace and all the trimmings!

Atlanta women, reading of "jet-colored frocks" were startled at this departure from the conventional ivory or white satin gown, particularly

ILLUSTRATION 266.

leading florists recalled a wedding he worked on where the bride elected black for her personal color scheme. Her gown was a black velvet dress with eggshell collar and cuffs. He considered it pretty, although unique. Having participated in weddings where the brides wore silver, gold, wine-color, blue, and green, this florist suggested that an all-black-and-white wedding might be interesting.[59]

Surely it was not only Atlanta women who took exception to the new fad. Any publication that carried advertising, particularly fashion magazines, showed women everywhere the designs of the season and the trends of the next.

Park Avenue's Powers models and the Ziegfeld girls of Hollywood became national symbols after 1938 as beauties and fashion mannequins who had attained the pinnacle of success. Powers models were "real people," known by their own names and personalities, but the remote, aloof models who wore expensive clothes created an unreachable image of sophistication. Dana Jenny, one of the latter, constantly appeared in the pages of *Harper's Bazar* and *Vogue* in the late 1930s. Debutantes' coming-out parties also stimulated curiosity in what was new; at the same time, magazines devoted to the styles of the day were more in demand than ever.

America's "haute couture" may have started with a label Hattie Carnegie put into a dress in 1924.[60] Assertive American designers continually enriched our national culture with innovative creations. Although American designers rose to international prominence in the thirties with the phenomenon of movies, many women still insisted on the French couturier. (The 1920s elite couldn't have existed without the Paris imports.) Two French designers in particular were well known: Coco Chanel and Jeanne Lanvin.

when they learned of a wedding costume fashioned of black velvet with a golden headdress and gilded lilies. "Such a costume would surely scare away the timid bridegroom," was the comment made by one Atlanta native.

In another account, an associate of one of the

ILLUSTRATION 267.

ILLUSTRATION 268.

ILLUSTRATION 269.

One of Lanvin's loveliest wedding gowns was inspired by the calla lily. It was made of heavy white silk crêpe. The low drapery at the hipline rolled back like the petals of the lily, and the trained skirt was long and slender like the stem. The veil was a round circle of net bordered with tiny pearls sewed on by hand. The bride carried calla lilies.[61]

A 1931 dress by Lanvin (Ill. 266) was made of ivory satin, with a "trained" spencer jacket. Beautiful in concept of design, the gown had the bias cut that made the satin mold to the body in a

ILLUSTRATION 270.

graceful, flowing line. The veil was point de venise lace over tulle. The bride carried calla lilies.

Much less sophisticated, yet cut along the same line, is the all-lace dress in Illustration 267. The lace was ingeniously cut on the bias to give a body-hugging look. In the front from knee to hem was a godet, an inverted "V," for fullness. The long lace train was cut circularly with only one center back seam. The gown had a small Peter Pan collar of the lace and fullness at the top of the sleeve, which tapered skin-tight from elbow to wrist. There were twenty-eight satin-covered buttons in front. The slip had a deep V-cut in back, almost to the waist, and a side zipper. To complete the costume, there was a

small cap of matching lace rimmed with a coronet of small fabric roses to which a long tulle veil was fastened.

Two gowns by well-known designers appeared in May 1931. One, a Worth gown in white brocade, was chosen by Princesse Isabelle d'Orleans-Brazance for her marriage to the Comte de Paris, at Palermo. The original was in pale pink satin, like the inside of a seashell. The train was cut long, into four panels, and the pale pink tulle veil was gathered into a cap beaded with crystal.

The other gown, by Molyneux, was very simple; made of white chiffon, it fell in long lines, sweeping the floor. The veil fit the head like a cap and spread to great width at the hem. A tiny

ILLUSTRATION 271.

ILLUSTRATION 272. *McCall pattern #8331.*

mother-of-pearl wreath encircled the head. The flowers were white butterfly orchids tied with a big satin ribbon bow and long streamers.

At a home wedding in Brownfield, Texas, early one morning in June 1930, the bride wore the sheer ecru georgette and lace dress shown in Illustrations 268 and 269. In the front there was a very wide, low inset of point d'Esprit lace overlaid with braid-outlined appliqués; this inset with an apron effect curved and rose to the natu-

ral waistline in back. Pink silk rose appliqués ornamented the raised waistline in the back and also decorated the upper right shoulder. The dress was worn over an ecru crêpe slip with a picoted, scalloped edge.

In the June 1932 wedding party shown in Illustration 270, the bride was wearing a white satin gown with a long train. There were chantilly lace sleeves, and the bride wore an orange blossom hat with a long net veil attached. American weddings for decades followed certain formal rules, exemplified by this 1932 photograph of the entire wedding party. In the prewar years, there was no thought of restraint in the quantity of laces, brocades, or silks, or of the huge flower sprays for the bride and all her female attendants. Free to exercise her own preferences, the bride could use as much of everything as she wished.

ILLUSTRATION 274.

ILLUSTRATION 273.

ILLUSTRATION 275.

ILLUSTRATION 276. *A 1938 magazine cover.*

ILLUSTRATION 277.

Apart from highly styled gowns, other elements of design in bridal attire existed for those who were very young or provincial, or those with no desire for slinky sophistication.

Hair styles of the 1930s were as varied as the gowns. Actresses on the stage and in the movies, who sported sleek styling, were very influential. A bride's hairdresser, or her mother, sister, or a friend, usually arranged her hair and headpiece, very early the day of the wedding. The short, controlled bob with marcel waves gave way to a longer, more romantic style. A pompadour hairdo, around 1934, evolved into attractive long styles, but was always curly. In 1937, the pageboy became popular. Permanent waves were universal, and soon commercial products allowed women to do a permanent wave at home.

Illustrations 271 and 273 show two wedding dresses (both worn in 1935) widely different in concept. The first (Ill. 271) is a white knit dress with hat, which the bride designed and knit herself. She was inspired by McCall's bridal pattern of that year (see Ill. 272) and made the dress accordingly. The matching hat made a completely coordinated picture.

The other gown (Ill. 273) is very girlish, light, and young, with yards and yards of white organdy. The short, puffed sleeves were very full. Organdy eyelet ruffle trimmed the square neckline, forming the collar; it also finished the short puffed sleeves and ornamented the entire hem, continuing around the long train. There were twelve yards of gathered eyelet ruffle around the hem and train. The only opening was an eleven-inch side zipper under the puffed sleeve. Illustration 274 shows the interesting treatment in the back, with the eyelet ruffle tapering down from the shoulder to side back at the waistline.

This style was actually called "the little-girl look." These girlish bridal dresses were youthful-looking mostly because of the material of which they were made. Eyelet and organdy dresses with peplums and short trains were popular with the young. (See the pinafore gown, Ill. 314.)

Seamstresses and designers enjoyed the luxury of the many varieties of goods available, from

ILLUSTRATION 278.

sheer organdies to satins, brocades, and silks. A product formerly called "artificial silk" was now given the name "Rayon."

Something exciting was to happen in the late 1930s. On October 27, 1938, the world of fashion had its initiation into synthetic fibers. With a formal announcement to the public, a synthetic creation called nylon was introduced to the world. Each ensuing year, lustrous, durable, and exciting man-made textiles from the world of chemistry and research were put into the hands of designers, couturiers, and fashioners. Wedding dress designers happily used these fabrics. Some were resilient and crisp; others held pleats and

creases and resisted wrinkling. Versatile Orlon acrylic was announced in 1944; Dacron polyester in 1946.[62]

The beautiful Hollywood actress and singer Jeanette MacDonald was one of 1937's most celebrated June brides. Her marriage to Gene Raymond took place on the cool summer night of June 16, in Hollywood. Many celebrities and friends filled the church. She wore a bridal creation designed by Adrian. (Illustration 275 is his original sketch.) The gown was made of rosy organza; the collar of duchesse lace with "point de gaze" lace was fastened with a posy. The overdress had leg-of-mutton sleeves and a long train; it was

ILLUSTRATION 279.

attached in front to the waist and opened on a slip-underskirt lined with taffeta. All edges were trimmed with loops of the same organza. The bonnet was made of the same lace as the collar, with a short net flounce edged with lace, trimmed at the nape of the neck with tiny flowers. The veil was voluminous, made of rosy white illusion tulle worn with the bonnet. This dress was exquisite in its dressmaking details.

The American bride of 1940 world stood at a crossroads in the world of fashion. Looking back two years, she could see that the outbreak of war in Europe had completely ended the abundant shipments of beautiful gowns from Paris and sister cities abroad. Political and military alliances, together with massive invasions of other nations, triggered a hideous war that touched her life in infinite ways. Yet, at the same time, she saw an America able to generate a festive atmosphere in its New York World's Fair of 1939–1940, and San Francisco's 1940 Golden Gate International Exposition. Still, America was gearing up for self-denial and an all-out war effort ahead.

Now it was time for the really creative American designers to turn to native sources of design for inspiration. The New York museums placed their treasures at the disposal of designers of clothing and textiles for study, with the result that American women from the late 1930s on were well dressed by their own talented designers. Los Angeles, as well as New York, became a leading center of dress and textile design.

Hattie Carnegie's apron fashions with dirndl skirts and peasant blouses revived an old fashion. In June 1940, she introduced a white Swiss embroidered apron and cap for a white organdy wedding dress and a pink and green plaid taffeta pinafore-apron for the bridesmaids. The aprons

ILLUSTRATION 280.

were removable. Armsful of field flowers gave a summery and picturesque look.

Linen, silk, and cotton were needed for war purposes, along with the new nylon; but the man-made fibers proved to be great favorites, never diminishing in popularity.

On May 15, 1940, nylon hosiery was offered for sale to the general public in stores throughout the country. (In October 1939, it had been put on sale to the public for the first time; distribution was limited to six stores in Wilmington, Delaware.) The quick-drying property of nylon stockings was a brand-new delight. By 1941, the material was being used for foundation garments, too.

Government regulations restricted the amount

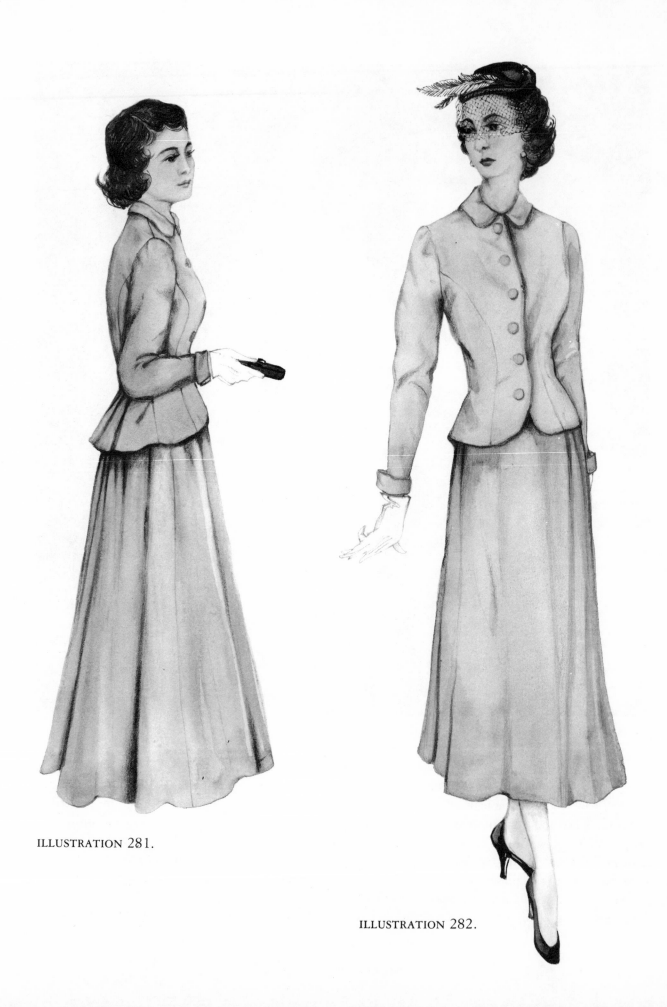

ILLUSTRATION 281.

ILLUSTRATION 282.

ILLUSTRATION 283.

of yardage a woman could use to make costumes during wartime. As a result, patterns discontinued balloon sleeves, cuffs, patch pockets, flaps on pockets, yokes, long suit jackets, hood capes, and sashes over two inches wide. Wedding dresses, however, were exempt from the ruling.

Still, many a bride learned to be practical, and celebrations were scaled down, somewhat reminiscent of the meager days of the depression. Young women, facing the challenge of restrictions, made wedding dresses that could be worn more than once, used remnants, and remade attractive clothing from used goods.

One young Polish-American couple had a small wedding in May 1943 (see Ill. 277). They regretted the fact that theirs was a small wedding, in sharp contrast to the wedding celebrations of their parents, which had included four days of feasting. The young couple instead had to face the facts of food rationing. Both bride and groom were employed at a company that made condensers for the Navy. The groom was not in uniform, as he was temporarily deferred from the army due to this essential work.

Fashions in 1942 magazines and newspapers showed brides wearing something both pretty and practical. One example was a dress of white rayon marquisette over taffeta, high-necked and long-sleeved. It had no train, but it did have a short jacket of white faille taffeta and a fingertip veil fastened to a bonnet. This formal style easily adapted to a cocktail or dinner dress.

The bride in Illustration 278 left the house in which she was born for her wedding in July 1940. Her father guided her through a line of ushers and bridesmaids showering confetti, streamers, pennies, nickels, and dimes. Neighborhood kids picked up the pennies and kept them, a custom in this New York neighborhood.

A black-haired beauty with soft blue eyes and flawless skin, debutante Brenda Frazier had a fashionable wedding in 1942. A beautiful woman can clothe herself in the plainest style without trimmings; simple attire actually enhances her beauty. Brenda Frazier's gown—a heavy satin with princess lines—was created by Herman Patric Tappé, of the House of Tappé. It had a bouffant skirt and sweeping train. The only lace bordered her hand bouquet of orange blossoms.

Many wartime weddings were held on brief notice in City Hall, in a magistrate's office, or in a minister's home or rectory. With the short fur-lough hours allotted to their grooms, brides did away with elaborate gowns and often wore suits, always with a hat, perhaps with a face veil that tickled the nose and chin.

The sweetheart neckline was used profusely. Found on dresses and blouses made of sheer materials, velvets, or brocades, it was becoming to almost everyone. The burgundy transparent-velvet dress and matching hat in Illustration 279 was chosen by a Mount Vernon, New York, girl for her October 1942 wedding. It, too, had the sweetheart neckline. The bride chose burgundy rather than white because of her strong feeling of patriotism; like her, many young women were willing to forego the traditional gown with train. Her dress and small shirred hat with face veil were bought at a fashionable Fifth Avenue shop in New York. The bride wore a white gardenia corsage and long white gloves.

The wartime bride had to be inventive. One clever idea for a headdress was to take grandmother's bridal handkerchief, drape it on the head, with one of the lacy points forming a heart-shaped effect in front. The veil was attached beneath the handkerchief, falling gracefully in back.

Illustration 280 shows a wartime wedding that held to tradition. The new husband helped his wife perform the ritual washing of the hands, which orthodox Jewish law requires before every meal (in this case, the wedding feast). The groom poured water from a cup over each of the bride's hands three times, then did the same for himself. This ended the religious ceremony for the bride and groom.

Finally, peace was declared, and the boys came home to be reunited with their loved ones. Many a marriage took place, and new freedom was reflected in all aspects of the ceremony. Designers once again knew the real joy and satisfaction of creating freely and moved in a new direction. With the deliberate goal of creating a new line and style, they shied away from anything resembling a military uniform. No more straight, broad shoulders, short skirts, red nails, red lips, or plucked and penciled eyebrows. A softer and more rounded female outline came into vogue.

Christian Dior did it best. In 1947, his stroke of line, which put the skirt down below the calf, was called "the new look." Seeing it for the first time, it seemed as if the woman were wrapped in a blanket from waist to ankle. Yet soon the new look was seen everywhere—by some with near-comic effect. Some winsome fashion features came with it, like an alluring softness with neat, trim midriff at the natural waistline, narrower shoulders (but padded and round), and a new emphasis on the bust.

The extremely long skirt of the new look did not last, except for formal and semiformal wear, when the ballerina-length and the cocktail-length skirt became popular. The decade ended with an easy style: pretty, short, and wide skirts and low décolleté bodices with a short bolero jacket. Hips were emphasized. A very slim skirt with flying panels was an elegant, almost theatrical innovation.

A gray velvet suit that typified the new look was worn by a bride who was married in the Gettysburg College chapel in October 1948 (see Ills. 281 and 282). The fitted jacket had a flared peplum and was fish-tailed in the back. There were six velvet-covered buttons. The skirt was ample and long.

In the same year (1948), a cotton velveteen dress of "heavenly blue" was worn over a blue taffeta petticoat and large hoop (see Ill. 283). The style of the dress pointed away from the severe wartime fashions to the crinoline hooped dresses of the next decade. The style was romantic, with a dropped shoulderline, full at the top and tapering to a point over the hand. The long, fitted waist, princess cut in front, was shaped to a point in back. Over the hoop was a heavy cording sewn *en tablieu* (apron style) across the front. The bonnet, made of the same blue velveteen, was in the Victorian mode, shirred and peaked in the center, and tied under the chin (see Ill. 228 in Chapter 11). The bride wore a cross necklace and carried two purple orchids over a steel-covered prayer book, which the groom had carried throughout the war while serving in the Corps of Engineers. The museum that has this dress and bonnet also has the pictures, bridesmaids' dresses, the "going away" suit, cocktail dress, and articles of clothing in the bridal trousseau.

Some gowns of this period presented very versatile combinations. One costume, designed to be worn for evening after serving as a wedding gown, was a basic dress of satin, cuffed bodice style, with slim, nipped-in waist and no train. For the wedding ceremony, a long-sleeved redingote of spidery lace was added, buttoned from the high neck to the low, pointed waistline with twenty-eight satin-covered buttons. The redingote, which parted at the center front waistline, was deeply gathered around the waist, then fell gracefully to the floor.

By 1949, much yardage was used in gowns. Yet the full-length bridal veil had all but disappeared from the scene.

16

Crinoline and Hoop Again: the Affluent 1950s

American fashion in the middle of the twentieth century was rich and didn't try to hide it. Formal and evening wear, wedding dresses, and other clothes all bespoke money and prosperity. The look took two distinct forms: the sophisticated and the youthful.

A 1950 Adele Simpson wedding suit, made of silk taffeta in a muted blue-gray tone, gave a sophisticated look in color and style and was an excellent choice for the wedding at home. Its hip-length jacket, nipped at the waist, had cuffed push-up sleeves and rounded revers (lapels) on the jacket. The full, gored skirt was banded with a wide, gathered cummerbund. With it, the model wore a sleeveless blouse of imported navy lace and a Sally Victor hat.

Another 1950 dress captured the very youthful

look. Starched and crisp, the organdy gown had a fitted bodice, a tiered skirt made of many layers of appliquéd organdy, and long sleeves.

Convertible bridal costumes were favored by many young women. Some dresses had a basque jacket that could be removed to show a strapless dress.

Wedding dresses retained tiny waists through the fifties, with the skirt billowing out over crinoline petticoats and hoops. The luxurious fabrics and voluminous skirts, which had been absent for so long, brought back with them another excessive style using yards and yards of rich materials.

In one beautiful, youthful design (created by Murray Hamburger in 1953), the lace bodice draped into an apron effect over the bouffant,

ILLUSTRATION 284.

ILLUSTRATION 285.

ILLUSTRATION 286.

verly Hills, California) shows the body outlined closely from bosom to hipline, then gently flaring to the floor with appropriate train. Made of cameo-tinted Italian silk, with a pearl embroidered skirt and jeweled hand-embroidered bodice, it had a white satin hoop underneath with a buckram foundation inside, at the hips. It was also accessorized by a tinted net veil, a jeweled silk headband, and tinted net hand mitts. It presented a very sophisticated look.

Ballerina length was the choice of many 1952 and 1953 brides. This was a skirt length about two to six inches above the ankle; it was also called cocktail length. For a summer wedding held in the beautiful setting of Orr's Island, Casco Bay, Maine, a gown of this length was chosen (see Ill. 285). The large floral bouquet was still used, even in the informal setting.

The fifties brought bridal dresses with wiring that made the high collar stand up along the neck in Elizabethan style. Fashion regularly follows current events, and the coronation of young Queen Elizabeth II in 1952 brought a revival of England's styles in both fashion and terminology. Long, pointed bodices (Tudor style), upstanding collars, jewels, tiaras, crowns, and farthingale pads inside skirts all reemerged in American fashion. The gown in Illustration 286 was of lace and nylon net with a stand-up collar. It had a very bouffant skirt with crinoline.

Tradition was too strong to allow many chemise-styled bridal gowns, cut straight and fairly tight from the armhole to the flank, without a waist. Active women, in their daily lives, wore the "siren sheath" chemise, as well as dungarees, shorts, and pedal pushers. For her wedding, however, the bride wanted a silhouette that showed a small waist, a high bosom, and a full skirt. These high-bosomed, beltless Empire gowns were made

hooped skirt. The lace was of hand-clipped Belgian lace. The skirt of white satin with double tiers of white nylon, gave it a filmy, ethereal appearance. Self-covered buttons on the waist were matched by about ten more on each sleeve to accentuate the pointed cuffs.

A gown of exquisite lace was made of a duplicated "French Calais lace," that mastery of craftmanship woven on the Leavers lace machine in France.

In 1952, some designers, anticipating an abundance of large skirts over crinoline, gave the figure a slimmer and softer silhouette (see Ill. 284). This dress (by William Cahill of Be-

ILLUSTRATION 287. *A taffeta and lace gown* (*c. 1952*).

with interlinings and feather-boning, which gave a delicate yet firm "body."

With the increasing popularity of short evening dresses, brides were finally persuaded to wear short street-length gowns, in elegant silk, taffeta, or lace.

Man-made fabrics enjoyed great popularity ever since their introduction, yet cotton was the chosen fabric for much of 1953's clothing. Dress designer Adele Simpson received the first annual Cotton Fashion Award from the Secretary of Agriculture, and the governmental stamp of approval was to continue. During World War II, also cotton was promoted as an intrinsic part of American life.

A Ceil Chapman creation was a work of art in cotton. Shown in the 1944 *New York Times* Fashion Show, it was acclaimed as "Cotton Queen," the hit of the show. Made of sheer, permanent-finish organdy, this wedding dress was cut on princess lines accented in exquisitely wrought scroll trimming of piqué appliqué. The scroll-like design of piqué was also stitched down the center of the full-length sleeves. A crinoline petticoat had a hoop sewn in eight inches from the bottom around the hem to display the beauty of the appliqué. This gown was also worn in a bridal show at the Hotel St. Regis in New York on January 9, 1945, honoring the American designers whose dresses appeared in *Brides* magazine during the year 1944.*

Genuine artistic mastery of dress designing shines in the 1955 wedding dress shown in Illustration 288. California designer James Galanos used skill in creating the beautiful gray lustrous silk. The close-fitting bodice had a low, square neckline with a high yoke drapery and small cap

*The gown may be found in the Costume Institute of the Metropolitan Museum of Art, New York.

ILLUSTRATION 288.

sleeves. At the tiny waist the skirt was gathered into one-eighth-inch pleats all around, giving a very bouffant look. In the front panel only, there were forty-six one-eighth-inch pleats. The material at the hem measured almost sixteen yards! The length of this dress echoed the evening length for that year, which Ceil Chapman called "shorter than long, longer than short," and Pauline Trigère called "intermission length."[63]

Fun fashions were popular in the late fifties, as sports events and more leisure-time activities allowed Americans to concentrate on clothing. Pleasure-oriented young Americans became ac-customed to wearing very casual clothes to affairs that previously would have demanded dressier styles. Some wedding gowns, mirroring this change, were made from Christian Dior's H-line style, a silhouette straight from shoulder to hip, crossed at the hip with a cuff or belt. Evening clothes took on a definite "back-sweep" line, as did wedding dresses.

Long and trained, the swept line in Illustration 289 fell from an Empire waist at center back, giving a regal appearance. The gown, with great simplicity of line, needed only the beaded embroidery scattered sparsely across the bodice and

ILLUSTRATION 289.

ILLUSTRATION 290.

ILLUSTRATION 291. *Detail of the guipure appliqué of the gown in Ill. 290.*

upper part of the skirt front for an artistic effect. The bateau neckline dipped to a low point in back.

Artist-designer Tamara Yohanan of San Francisco presented the wedding dress in Illustration 290, in fall 1959. It was made of heavy oyster-white satin; the sleeveless bodice had a deep pleated bertha flounce around the rounded neckline. The narrow skirt had two pleated flounces of self-material and in front were two appliqué wreaths of heavy guipure (heavy lace with a large pattern) with crystal crops and pearls.

In the last part of the decade, French designers created inspired fashions, some of which were intensely dramatic. Balenciaga and Givenchy, with individual styling of the "sack silhouette," were among them. That sack silhouette was almost like a giant almond with sleeves, seeming to muffle the natural human shape. Some gowns barely touched the hips, then tapered to a narrow hem just below the knee. Most had beautiful dressmaking details.

American designers showed great proficiency at inventing new styles. Claire McCardell's "string bean" silhouette and Estevez's spectacularly revealing necklines gave rise to a trend: semifitting sheaths with bare, strapped necklines. Some designers blended the sack and the sheath by using a loose, straight overdress of transparent fabric to veil the shapely underdress.

Brides of the 1950s were married in an affluent decade. Luxurious fabrics and styles combined to create a decided air of quality. This was a period of good taste in styling, sophistication, some girlishness, and many beautiful creations for the bride.

17

The Dramatic Bride
and the Military Bride

Every age has brides with a flair for drama. Some young women envision their wedding as a day of grandeur and plan to add drama to the ceremony with a unique gown. Sometimes the results are crazes, such as the svelte black satin bridal gown of the 1930s or the disposable paper dresses in the sixties.

In fact, for literal drama, an organization called the Society for Creative Anachronism, whose purpose is to study the customs and culture of the Middle Ages by recreating them, has staged some truly dramatic weddings. Ceremonies have been held in which the bride and groom wear wedding garments made in the medieval or Renaissance style. The costumes are often spectacular.

Two assistant math teachers at the University of Texas had a wedding in March 1977 held in the garden of the Laguna Gloria Art Museum with full-dress Renaissance bridal attire. The bride's sister, a lute player who was involved in medievalist activities in San Francisco, carried the bride's train. The traditional vows were read in Latin. The celebration was complete with a wandering minstrel and a full-size, meatless Lenten feast. Photographs and story appeared in the student newspaper at the university.[64]

Guests who attended the December 31, 1983, wedding of a young couple were taken back to fourteenth and seventeenth centuries. The bridal dress of 1300 was known as a *cotehardie;* it had a tightly fitted bodice, laced at the back or buttoned up the front (see Ill. 292). Often lined with fur, the gowns had jeweled bands around the

ILLUSTRATION 292.

ting was used at this early date to give a raised look to the fabric, and bells were often sewn on a garment. England's sumptuary laws strictly forbade the use of ermine and pearls to those who did not possess a thousand pounds yearly income. Frisé—a precious cloth of gold—silver, jewel embroidery, and miniver and other furs were forbidden those not having a yearly income of 400 marks.

As faithful to the style and custom as was possible, this young bride of 1983 used fifty-three gold ball buttons on the front of her fitted bodice. She used a gold and silver braid trim for the belt and girdle, and the dress itself was a white brocade with gold-flecked design. The low bateau neckline had a fur trim with black hearts like jewels embedded in it. The sleeves were separate from the gown and made of a metallic gold cloth with floral design in white. On the edges of the sleeves the bride sewed tiny silver bells, as did all the girls in the wedding party. The bride also appliquéd clover-shaped tatting to the bottom of her dress. Pearls, too, were used as ornaments at the hem.

The bride's medieval name is Lady Suzanna of the House of Jewels; the groom's, Sir Tokomak Te' Abbata Sarran. His wedding costume was a 1625 French cavalier outfit. What a dramatic picture they presented at this 1983 candlelit ceremony!

Sometimes brides got their ideas for drama from outside influences, such as travel to another country where something in the culture was especially desirable. Some actually copied a costume fashionable in another country. Boutiques and specialty shops have offered distinctive styles and provided variety.

A 1970 Texas bride and her attendants wore gowns inspired by another time. The wedding

neck and the hips. A jeweled or leather belt was worn on which to hang objects such as pouches, knives, and mirrors. Necklines in this period were low, exposing the shoulders. Since ladies' sleeves were used as pennants on the lances of faithful knights, they were made separate from the dress, even of a different color. Several pairs of sleeves might be made for one gown; ladies were always prepared to give them away as favors. Tat-

ILLUSTRATION 293. *Egyptian influence on a bridal costume.*

ILLUSTRATION 294. *A scene from a 1929 production of* The Taming of the Shrew, *with Mary Pickford and Douglas Fairbanks.*

gown was a chalk-white classic of double-faced crêpe in a flowing line, caught at the waist by a white braided satin rope belt with silk tassels. The large trumpet sleeves were also trimmed with tassels. The headdress brought back a Middle Ages look: a high, rolled collar and form of amice* covered her neck, shoulder, and the side of her head and was fastened to the high band of the headdress; from this fell the long sheer veil. A large gold cross was worn in pendant fashion.

Her attendants were equally dramatic, wearing bright orange sleeveless togas with high stand-up collars and sandals. These tunics zipped up the back and were split to the waist on either side to reveal mortar-colored culottes. The Empire-style waists were accented with braided grosgrain rib-

bon sashes in bright pink, green, old gold, orange, and pale pink. Entwined in the braids in the bridesmaids' hair were ribbons that streamed down the center of the back. These ribbons repeated the colors in the sashes.

As we have seen, the strong influence of prominent personalities here and abroad has stimulated designers to emulate them. Princess Margaret's wedding in 1960 roused interest and renewed curiosity about past royal weddings, as did Princess Elizabeth's in 1947 and Princess Diana's in 1981. The wedding finery of Marie Louise, who became Napoleon's second wife in 1810, is a historical treasure. She wore an Empire gown of crimson satin embroidered in gold, with white pearls at the front. The court train was lined in ermine. This royal gown has inspired contemporary designers to make similar versions. One adaptation was a gown with a high-belted waistline, embroidered with sprays of pearls and sequins, just as the original.

Around 1952, Christian Dior introduced a new Elizabethan silhouette. Its essence was a dramatic gown of ivory moiré with hips padded in farthingale line. When given free reign to execute their dreams, designers can come up with sensational creations, unique and often fleeting.

Reflection of an African heritage evoked a particularly interesting design (1970) in a brocaded bridal caftan (see Ill. 295). Accented with silver braid, it had a matching turban.

Setting often has a great deal to do with a spectacular wedding. A rambling stone estate in the Blue Ridge foothills of Virginia was the setting for one bride's all-white wedding. Part of the drama was the combination of traditional elements of both Virginia and Scotland, the parents' homeland. The wedding was endowed with a special meaning and charm, for both history and

*An oblong linen vestment worn about the neck and shoulders, similar to a scarf.

ILLUSTRATION 295.

ILLUSTRATION 297.

ILLUSTRATION 296.

sentiment recalled the Scottish heritage in a blending of wedding motifs of Scotland and Virginia.

The bride's dress of ivory linen had a wide panel of guipure lace descending down the front, the cuffs, and the standing collar. A high conical crown headpiece came together in a clutch of tulle. At the neck of her gown the bride pinned the family brooch, a precious heirloom crafted on the island of Iona in an old, symbolically heart-shaped Celtic design. The brooch was topped with the crown of Mary, Queen of Scots. The bridal bouquet was a crescent-shaped white cascade of roses, carnations, and heather. White heather is a powerful symbol of good luck in Scotland. It is very rare there and does not exist in America at all; lavendar heather was frosted white for the occasion.

Each bridesmaid wore a different tartan sash, gathered at the shoulder of her white linen gown with a silver Scottish pin. The wedding party echoed the Gaelic theme that characterized the entire affair.[65]

In the 1930s, 1940s, and 1950s, Americans flocked to provincial little productions held in schools, churches, town halls, or small theaters. Called the Tom Thumb wedding, it featured four and five-year-olds dressed in carefully detailed bridal clothes to simulate an adult wedding. Nonprofessional and nonprofit groups went to

ILLUSTRATION 298.

ILLUSTRATION 299.

ILLUSTRATION 300.

great effort to stage these elaborate productions (see Ill. 296).

The idea of a wedding "in miniature" stemmed from the actual wedding of two Little People, General Tom Thumb and Lavinia Warren (see Ill. 297). Their marriage in Grace Church, New York, was showered with publicity. Two tiny friends, Commodore Nutt and Minnie Warren, served as best man and bridesmaid.

When he was four years old, Tom was discovered in Bridgeport, Connecticut, by P. T. Barnum, who billed him as General Tom Thumb and took him on tour. He was a smash hit wherever he went. Barnum took him on a three-year European tour and raised his salary to $50 a week. An 1844 critic described a typical audience: "They push, they fight, they scream, they faint. I would not have believed it of the English people." Even Queen Victoria requested three command performances. In Paris, Tom's success was even greater. Barnum had to take a cab every night to carry home his bag of silver earned by the tiny performer.[66]

Tom Thumb and his wife Lavinia were still performing with Barnum and Bailey in 1881, at the age of forty-one; but P. T. Barnum was not the first to know and use the name Tom Thumb for a Little Person. In one of his twelve volumes, English novelist and playwright Henry Fielding included a drama about Tom Thumb, first acted in 1730. English storytellers have kept alive the account through the years, and in our own libraries we can find illustrated storybooks of this delightful fairytale in *The Adventures of Tom Thumb*.

Almost everyone has known of at least one dramatic and fascinating wedding. Creativity is at its best in diversity, and human imagination is a vital part of the art of designing.

The Military Bride

There is no way we could leave the military wedding out of our connubial overview. Rich with ritual and dignity, its elegance leaves a lasting impression. Dress uniforms vary with the time of year or the time of day, making a sharp contrast to the bride's white gown and veil. Other regulations and the ceremonial customs of each branch of the service lend color and flair to the occasion. Formality and convention rule a military wedding, with the highlight being the "Arch of Swords" (navy and marine corps) or the "Arch of Sabers" (army and air force.) The variations among the services are subtle as to commands, format, and settings; however, the arch beneath which the uniformed groom and his bride pass, to be presented to family, friends, and the military community, remains a constant. It is a spectacular drama, joining the ringing military commands with the wedding rite. The regalia of military dress uniforms and pageantry complement the bride's beauty with sophistication and splendor. The camaraderie and custom of the military wedding—the crisp presence of the uniformed groom and groomsmen, the ceremonial arch of swords or sabers—bring the bride into the "military family."

Wartime is not the only time military weddings are practiced. As long as the groom and groomsmen are authorized to wear military uniform, the ceremony may take place in times of peace as well.

Many times a military wedding must take place at a base chapel far from the bride's home, or even in another country. All arrangements are made long distance by phone and mail in these situations.

Illustration 298 shows an 1899 bride photographed with her attendant, groom, and groomsmen. Seven of the men, including the groom, were uniformed members of the U.S. Army. The wedding took place six months after the end of the Spanish-American War, in Skaneateles, New York. Major John J. Pershing (who later became a general) was one of the ushers.

Fort Hamilton's first all-military wedding took place at the Post Chapel on Easter Sunday, 1944 (see Ill. 299). The bride, a private, wore the traditional white gown, the current style of the day. The groom was a sergeant.

George Washington, a distinguished Virginian, was a young colonel when he met the widow Martha Dandridge Custis, a young Virginia matron, and offered her his hand. They planned to marry in January 1759, presumably at the Custis home in Kent County, known as the "White House."

In the Virginia capital at Williamsburg and in the homestead of every plantation for miles around, the preparation for the nuptials of Colonel Washington and Martha Custis had been the theme of many gatherings during the Christmas holidays of 1758. In her girlhood the bride had been one of the belles of Williamsburg society, and there was no country gentleman along the Potomac who was not familiar with the colonel's excellence as a horseman, hunter, and soldier.

The road to the "White House" that midwinter morning was bright with the gaiety and glitter of little groups of beautifully dressed neighbors. Washington himself enjoyed the elegant observances of ceremony and rich attire, and no colonial bridegroom had graced a wedding with more stately dignity. He stood six feet two inches tall, with a slender, tapering frame. He was athletic, with broad shoulders and hips; neatwaisted but not deep-chested. He had blue-gray, penetrating eyes, round cheekbones, and his dark brown hair was done up in a queue.

As he enjoyed fashionable clothing, he had traveled to Philadelphia, New York, and Boston in the finest apparel of his military rank, and the English tailor from whom he imported his ordinary clothing had no more precise customer in describing the details and the fashion of his garb as ordered. The clothes in which he was married undoubtedly came from London. He had ordered from abroad "as much of the best superfine blue cotton velvet as will make a coat, a waist-coat and breeches for a tall man, with a fine silk button to suit it, six pairs of the very neatest shoes, and other articles of a gentleman's outfit."

In a suit of blue and silver with scarlet trimmings, a waistcoat of white satin, embroidered, buckles of gold on his knee garters and shoes, his hair powdered, and by his side a straight dress sword, the bridegroom towered above most of his companions. His bride did not reach higher than his shoulders when she stood beside him before the old Episcopal clergyman in his full canonicals.

The bride also wore a costume from London: a heavy white silk, shot with silver, which was worn over a white satin quilted petticoat. In her hair and ears were pearl ornaments. She wore white satin slippers, and on the buckle of each was a diamond. She wore the ring the bridegroom had ordered for her in Philadelphia at the time of their engagement.

The young matron, twenty-six years old, had brown hair and hazel eyes, a plump and pleasing figure, and an easy, graceful carriage. There were three bridesmaids, all charming Virginia women. The distinguished country gentlemen in their fine raiment and the provincial officers from Williamsburg in their uniforms were headed by Lieutenant-Governor Fauquier, who was brilliant in a uniform of scarlet cloth embroidered in gold. He wore a bag-wig, a current fashion, and carried a dress sword. Around him stood a group of English officers, together with members of the legislature and other civilians.

When the bride entered the coach, bright with the Washington colors of red and white, and drawn by six horses guided by black postilions in livery, the bridegroom did not enter with her. His tall body-servant was holding the reins of his favorite horse, waiting for him to mount. After Washington mounted the well-bedecked charger, he rode by the side of the bridal coach, closely followed by a cortège of gentlemen on horseback.

Those were not the days of brief or informal weddings; and this wedding, with London liveries and London gowns, was no doubt a social occasion marked with even more than the customary Virginia hospitality and merriment. Every kinsman, friend, and neighbor was expected to take part in the festivity, and the house was filled with kinspeople enjoying the feast and revelry.[67]

In another celebration, a newlywed bestows a kiss upon his bride beneath the traditional crossed sabers (see Ill. 300); this privilege is accorded to graduates of West Point who have just been married at the cadet chapel.

Modern couples treasure the memories and the photographs that capture the dramatic moment of passing beneath the military arch.

18

The Liberated Bride:
Going to Extremes (1960s-1980s)

The 1960s were a time of political and social upheaval. Looking back over the decade, powerful and overwhelming memories linger. We can remember denims, long hair, miniskirts, the Twiggy influence, beehive hairdos, nudity, paper throwaways, Mary Quant and the Mods, and Woodstock.

Where did the bride find herself in all this diversity? She found that she was free to go to extremes, free from inherited convention. The bride transcends the times in which she lives; her history of what she wore supersedes what the fashion designers have said she should wear.

The hippie bride's dress was decidedly individual. Although the majority of sixties brides were not hippies, yippies, or women who practiced the extremes of fashion, some were

definitely influenced by those life-styles. But though youth cult fashions thrived, some women still chose the traditional wedding.

At a September wedding in New York City in 1964, the bride wore a long, white bridal dress of doubled organdy, from the House of Christian Dior, made in Paris (see Ill. 301). The slim, shoe-top-length dress had white bell-shaped passementerie, hand-applied, and beading in a floral motif on lower skirt and lower sleeves. The dress was worn by Mary Josephine McFadden, former director of public relations with Dior–New York.

Diverse and freely selected styles in wedding gowns were chosen. Such famous women as Jacqueline Kennedy were followed and copied; it was the fashionable Mrs. Kennedy who was partly

ILLUSTRATION 301.

ILLUSTRATIONS 302 & 303. *A taffeta and lace miniskirt with a bridal boutique label:* Bridal Originals.

responsible for the vogue of the high-bosomed, princess dress, without sleeves or belt. No one wore it more magnificently than she. Young designers such as Donald Brooks, who won a Coty American Fashion Critics' Award for outstanding creative influence, and Norman Norell were highly influential.

Hollywood designer James Galanos (considered a Californian although born in Philadelphia) had an unusual aptitude for fine construction and beautiful detailing. A tunic-shaped wedding dress of basket-weave synthetic fiber was included in his 1966 collection. Made of a raffia mesh cage covered with white embossed linen flowers, the dress had a short flaring train and a hat to match. It was valued at $3,500 that year.*

Wigs, wiglets, and false hair were widely—and openly—used in the 1960s, particularly by brides. Some women used falls or glamor curls to add a romantic touch to short hair; a small hair fill-in piece cost from $1.29 to $400, with a choice of over a hundred colors.

Young Americans love fads. In 1967, along with the micromini skirt and the unisex fashions, the disposable garment was a hit. As a result, a few wedding dresses were made of paper!

Anthony L. Muto of New York designed the dress in Illustration 306, made of white waffle-textured paper. It featured the A-line and long,

*From the costume collection of the Los Angeles County Museum of Art, CA.

ILLUSTRATION 304. *With the subtlest shaping of the long line, this well-designed dress (1968) by Gustave Tassell is made of ivory silk moiré and comes with a hood. It is in the A-line coat style, with a hidden button closure in center front.*

ILLUSTRATIONS 305 & 306. *A disposable paper wedding dress (1967).*

ILLUSTRATION 307. *A Qiana wedding dress.*

set-in sleeves; the cuffs and hem were trimmed with a deep border of white and ivory three-dimensional paper carnations and crysan-themums. The veil is white nylon net, gathered at the center into a bunch of three-dimensional white paper carnations with an attached comb. When the hands are joined, the cuffs of flowers form a muff.

Man-made fabrics, practical and attractive, quickly found a way into the world market. Top American fashion designers, in concert with fash-ion models and fashion magazines, have been in-volved with such fabrics almost since the man-made fibers were introduced commercially. One unique creation was a material called Qiana in-troduced by DuPont in 1969. Fabrics made from Qiana nylon offered a softness, depth, and bril-liance of color and visual clarity previously ap-proached only by the finest silks. At the same time, the fabric also had the performance charac-teristics associated with today's best man-made fibers. Although giving the appearance of silk, Qiana garments are strong and can hold their body and shape. Ideal for wedding dresses, many lovely Qiana creations have made their way "down the aisle."

That trip down the aisle may be a long time in the making. One mother spent two years making a dress for her daughter, crocheting an "old-fashioned" hooped wedding dress from soft, yet durable, washable and mothproof yarn. This dress, which was to be stored for future genera-tions, was crocheted of Orlon and decorated with tiny seed pearls for a finishing touch (see Ill. 308).

Despite campus revolts, contempt for author-ity, live-ins, and the Viet Nam protests swirling around her, a prospective bride still sought out her own path.

ILLUSTRATION 308. *A crocheted Orlon dress with hoop.*

By the 1970s, Lady Fashion was vulnerable enough to have been pushed in all directions; many beautiful young women took delight in abusing her when she proclaimed a style should be "precisely this, unequivocally, for this season." These beauties, models, and the girls in the office looked at her designs but often lifted their chins and stayed out of her doorway. They had deter-mined minds of their own and intended to have

exactly what they liked and what was most becoming to them. Of course, Lady Fashion influenced them constantly.

The need for total self-expression in clothing was—and is—most evident in the planning of the wedding dress, the bride's one day to solo. As the dress proclaimed the kind of woman she really was, why not put into it a bit of drama, innocence, or luxury? Even a young woman indifferent to all other fashions wanted her wedding dress to say something special. Since the woman of the seventies was free to express herself, we find much variation in styling and line. Frothy creations intrigued certain brides who had to have a "dream-come-true" dress. Filmy sheers and yards of lace satisfied a childhood image of a princess bride. Designers and manufacturers supplied the reality.

One 1972 version of the dream clothes the bride in tiers of Chantilly lace with a sweeping train. The sleeves billowed out full in the Gibson Girl style. Choosing deep, vibrant colors for her bridesmaid and attendants, the bride, in white, kept herself center stage.

Many college girls and career girls of the 1970s chose to wear the 1950s dresses their mothers wore on their wedding day—provided they could fit into the tiny waistlines! They did not want to put hundreds of dollars into a gown that would be worn one day only.

In America, generations ago, women had names like Samantha, Abigail, Hetty, Isabella Jane, Molly, or Prudence. In the 1960s, seventies, and eighties, girls had names like Megan, Cheri, Jean, Donna, Holly, Lauren, and Courtney. We find these names among the young

ILLUSTRATION 309. *An ivory chiffon chemise by Barbara, for Murray Hamburger.*

ILLUSTRATION 310. *A wedding at home. The gown is by Piccione. (Photograph by Richard Ballarian.)*

ILLUSTRATION 311.

ILLUSTRATION 312.

ILLUSTRATION 313.

ILLUSTRATION 314.   ILLUSTRATION 315.

women wearing the lovely bridal gowns featured in this chapter—the brides of the late twentienth century.

Jean designed her own wedding dress, a romantic-looking gown in pale blue chiffon, in her junior year in art school. After graduation the following year, she wore it for her September wedding. On the blue chiffon are rows and rows of lace and pearls. The bodice has soft shirring; five layers of chiffon form the skirt. The gown was photographed for a newspaper article headlined "The New Romantics—gowns by top student designers."[68]

Fond of 1920s styles, prospective brides had a growing market to accommodate them. Illustration 309 shows a 1920s chemise of ivory chiffon,

ILLUSTRATION 316.

ILLUSTRATION 317.

ILLUSTRATION 318.

ILLUSTRATION 319.

ILLUSTRATION 321.

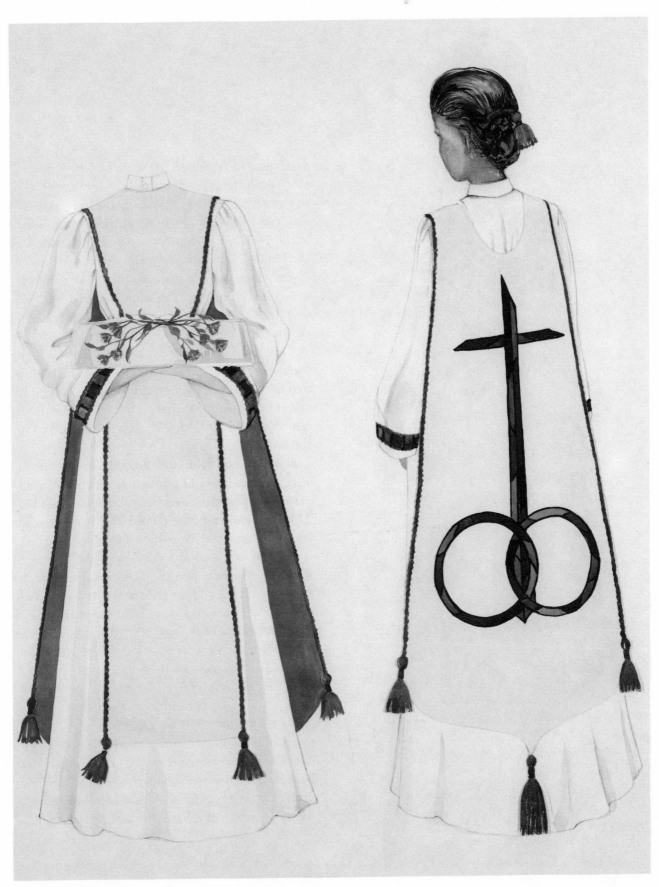

ILLUSTRATION 320.

ILLUSTRATION 322.

flounced and ribboned. Alençon lace ripples on a two-tiered hem and is repeated beneath the squared neckline and shoulder-touching sleeves. The big-brimmed hat with yards of chiffon (by Marie of T & G Bridal) was a suitable frame for the face.

For her own home wedding a comfort-conscious woman might wear a ruffled peau de soie dress trimmed with a band of turquoise velvet and pearled Alençon lace (see Ill. 310).

Three generations of a California family kept the bonds of treasured memories alive with photographs and cherished gowns (see Ills. 311, 312, and 313). Spanning the years of the twentieth century, from 1902–1972, each bride adhered to the mode of the day.

Standing straight and stately, the bride of 1902 wore a dress of white silk albatross* with narrow vertical tucking from yoke to floor (see Ill. 311). A double ruffle circled the hemline and another about twelve inches above the hem. A three-inch sash tied in a flat bow at the left front waistline. Bishop sleeves were finished with a five-inch cuff. The hair style was soft and waved around the face with a bun on the top of the head, where a white ribbon bow nestled just to the left front. Her slippers were a soft white kid with two-and-a-half-inch heels, a strap across the instep, and a circle of blue forget-me-nots on the toes.

For their June 1949 wedding, the next generation's bride wore the current waltz-length gown (see Ill. 312), popularized by Hollywood star Rita Hayworth when she married Ali Kahn. The dress, of reembroidered panels of white mousseline de soie, had a V-neck, inset cummerbund,

---

*A lightweight worsted fabric with a crêpe or pebble finish (or a soft nap surface).

ILLUSTRATION 323.

ILLUSTRATION 324.

and cap sleeves. With the short sleeves, long white lace mitts were worn to cover bare shoulders; the mitts had slit fingers for rings, which were of rubies and diamonds. The veil was of French illusion, and she carried an orchid fastened to a prayer book.

In a pose that duplicated that of her grandparents, the 1972 bride wore a gown of white peau d'ange (see Ill. 313), which had one individual feature that was a favorite hallmark of the forthcoming bicentennial in 1976: the dust ruffle. This gown had a very full skirt over an equally full, stiffened petticoat. The leg-of-mutton sleeves were gathered into a triple row of lace at the wrist, similar to lace edging at the high neck. Her headband of velvety white roses, lilies of the valley, and stephanotis was similar to the bouquet of real flowers that she carried. This bouquet contained red roses, two of which were given to the mothers as part of the ceremony and, as it was a December wedding, the bouquet included some holly from the family garden. The couple exchanged ruby and diamond rings, which had become a family tradition.

The dust ruffle, so popular around the time of the bicentennial celebration of 1976, was used on formal gowns as well as country-style pinafores. One (see Ill. 314), which did not even skim the floor, had the country-apron look in a charming white cotton and polyester eyelet. The square-throated pinafore style was flounced at the hem. It was worn over a long-sleeved green velvet dress.

First worn in 1899, the gown in Illustration 315, of handsome Brussels lace in stylized floral design, again graced a bride in 1982. Its style is modified late-nineteenth century in princess line with a slight train.

ILLUSTRATION 325. *This September 1984 bride chose a white gown of organza and silk schiffli embroidery with a cape bodice and crown collar with sheer, triangular yoke. The peacock-style, chapel-length train was attached to the crown collar of the dress. The picture hat, trimmed with seed pearls and miniature pink rosebuds, completes the romantic look.*

Lauren used complete self-expression as she celebrated her wedding with a weekend of festivities, sharing with friends and relatives in conversation, good food, and joyous celebration at a beach resort. But for the brief ceremony, bride, groom, and pastor wore long robes with ecclesiastical symbols printed on the fabric (see Ill. 316). The school art teacher executed the designs, no easy task. The bride made the robes, hers from a natural homespun with a warm golden yellow for the design. The groom's was orange with dark red for the design, and the pastor's was purple, accented with deeper mauve. All three robes had attached hoods.

A word should be said about the symbolism called on throughout the whole event. The capuchin was a hooded cape, a survivor of the sixteenth-century garment worn by friars in Italy in 1525. It symbolized a return to the original high-minded spirituality and the austere simplicity of the rule of St. Francis of Assisi.

Lauren, slender and pretty, made a winsome picture in her simplicity, for she wore no shoes and carried no flowers or book. Since from the earliest times the bride has always had "something to carry," this bride carried herself, gracefully and well.

At second marriages brides usually have more than ample resources from which to choose something to wear. For spring or summer second weddings, 1977 brought a vast selection of long, sheer floral prints. The one in Illustration 317 was the choice for a May bride, most becoming to her with its cardinal sleeves edged with lace. Two lace bands surrounded the skirt, waist, and V-neck, and the bodice and sleeves were finely tucked.

Despite leeway for individuality, surveys throughout the seventies show that the very traditional white wedding dress, veil and bouquet was chosen most often. Donna Marie selected her beautiful gown from the style trend of 1976 for her wedding in July 1977 (see Ill. 318).

Combining self-expression, a generous amount of artistic taste, and the added dimension of devotion appropriate to a reverent wedding ceremony, the designer of the ensemble in Illustrations 319 and 320 executed every garment in the wedding party by hand. The outer hanging was worn only during the ceremony, and then removed. Made of a natural, textured blend, it was bordered by a deep blue yarn braid, finished with tassels. The back displayed the Christian wedding symbol done in crewel embroidery in six bright rainbow colors of tapestry yarn. The lining was a lustrous gold. The white even-weave cotton dress had long, loose sleeves, finished with the crewel embroidery at the cuff and a belt of rainbow colors. Instead of flowers, blue silk bachelor's buttons were fastened to a hymn board.

The groom's attire (see Ill. 321), in harmony with this ensemble, was a long overshirt of white cotton, with a crewel embroidery band at the neckline and a tasseled purple yarn belt at the waist.

It is interesting to note that the designer used an 1890 treadle machine to sew the garments for this 1977 affair. Of course, the buttonholes were all done by hand, as were the trimming and other details.

Holly had a special admiration for the exquisite handiwork of Mexican women, so when she planned her December 1977 wedding, she searched for a dress with this fine craftmanship. In Tucson, Arizona, she found the beautiful white, all-cotton tucked dress with peasant embroidery shown in Illustration 322. The peasant "bib," attached to the front of the bodice and the shoulders, was decorated with colorful embroidery. There was a high stand-up collar of lace and cotton. The sleeves of fine vertical tucks were full, with deep, tight cuffs horizontally tucked and closed with three wooden buttons and an embroidered, diamond-shaped panel in the center of each sleeve. The skirt was made of six panels of fine tucks, each seam section finished with satin ribbon and lace. The skirt ended in a deep, twelve-inch ruffle, with six triangular floral-embroidered insets above it. The stitchery was done in variegated pink-red-maroon cotton yarn, also golden yellow and hunter green. The bride wore satin ribbons in her hair that matched the colored yarns of the flowers. These streamers fell from the psyche knot on top of her head. Her bouquet, in nosegay form, had red and gold roses, holly, evergreens, and baby's breath.

Cheri could have bought a very costly, fine gown, but since she loved to sew and was full of creative ideas, she decided to make her own wedding dress (see Ill. 323). Although busy with college studies, she found time to begin sketching a design. She had been inspired by a wedding dress pattern in one of the style books of the year. Like many inventive women, she only partially followed the classic design from the pattern, using her own ideas for variation.

The back of a bride's dress is often viewed as much as the front, especially as she slowly proceeds down the aisle. Here the dress hem was changed to produce a sort of bustle; the ruffle extended in circular form and caught up at center back near the waistline. The ruffles were all cut on the bias.

Much of the beauty of this gown was in the fabric: the body of the gown was polyester satin and the outer fabric angel-wing polyester chiffon. The bride designed and made the entire costume, even the fourteen tiny covered buttons, the veil, and the bonnet. The daisies, carnations, and baby's breath she carried added to the quaint look of this bridal gown, which Cheri wore for her August 1977 wedding.

Young designers of the 1980s contribute innovative new creations to the long procession of American brides. A young Philadelphia designer and dressmaker has created the dress in Illustration 324 for a November 1984 wedding. Wrapped and tied with a bow, the bride's dress is made entirely of white silk satin. Although the train is attached, the shoulder piece is removable and leaves a sophisticated, strapless, princess-line ball gown for late-night waltzing.

Modern American wedding dress designers have the distinct advantage of drawing upon centuries of styles for the bride. They are free to choose any color or line, wildly casual or highly sophisticated styles. Yet the designers stay within traditional limits. The great majority of brides still look for a costume that is white and formal, embellished with lace and beads. The popularity of the picture hat still continues throughout the 1980s.

We have seen all shapes, sizes, and colors of America's wedding dresses through the ages. Whether formal or casual, old-fashioned or highly contemporary, handmade or purchased, passed on through generations or worn only once, they all have one thing in common: they bring out the beauty of our country's women and truly say, "Here comes the bride!"

Identification and Acknowledgment of Illustrations

CHAPTER 1

ILL. 1. Photograph by Robert Wallace of oil painting on canvas, entitled *The Wedding,* by Eanger Irving Couse (1866–1936), in the collection of Harrison Eiteljorg, Indianapolis Museum of Art, Indianapolis.

ILL. 2. Drawing by author from description and illustration of Indian hair dressing. From *America's Fascinating Indian Heritage* (Reader's Digest Publication) p. 208.

ILL. 3. Photograph in an album compiled by Evaline E. Bentley. Album is in the Arizona Historical Society, Tucson.

ILL. 4. Drawing by author from dress style, c. 1501, in the painting by Jacques von Laethem in the Musée des Beaux Arts, Brussels, Belgium. From *Henry VIII and His Wives Paper Dolls* (San Francisco: Bellerophon Books)

ILL. 5. Drawing by author of Spanish-style dress of Eleanor of Portugal, from a fresco by Pinturicchio in the Library at Sienna. From *Henry VIII and His Wives Paper Dolls* (San Francisco: Bellerophon Books)

ILL. 6. Drawing by author of an English-style dress, c. mid-1500s; from a painting (artist unknown) of Queen Elizabeth as an adolescent.

ILL. 7. Steel engraving of Lady Jane Grey, c. 1553, from *Ridpath's History of the World,* vol. 5, p. 272.

ILL. 8. Drawing by author of the style of dress (simplified) worn by Queen Mary I; from paintings, c. 1554.

ILL. 9. Drawing by author of one style of ruff, mid-sixteenth century, from paintings and contemporary drawings (Mary Stuart, Catherine de Medici, Mary Tudor).

ILL. 10. Original woodcut (1982) by Phyllis Clark

Harvey, graphic designer, Wilmington, Delaware.

ILL. 11. Drawing by author of the style of dress worn by Mrs. Forrest and her maid, Anne Burroughs, first English woman to be married on American soil—1608. Description of dress from *History of the First Discovery and Settlement of Virginia*, by William Stith. The illustration is redrawn from Fig. 21, illustration by Sophie B. Steele, 1902. From the book *History of American Costume, 1607–1870*, by Elisabeth McClellan (New York: Tudor Publ. Co., 1937)

ILL. 12. Drawing by author.

ILL. 13. *The Marriage of Priscilla*, courtesy of the Bettmann Archive, Inc., NY.

ILL. 14. Drawing by author from *Five Centuries of American Costume* by R. Turner Wilcox (New York: Charles Scribner's Sons, 1963), p. 118.

ILL. 15. Drawing by author from *Five Centuries of American Costume* by R. Turner Wilcox (New York: Charles Scribner's Sons, 1963), p. 119.

ILL. 16. *Wedding in New Amsterdam*, courtesy of the Bettmann Archive, Inc., NY.

ILL. 17. Drawing by author of style of dress c. 1660, of English and Dutch origin.

CHAPTER 2

ILL. 18. Style of dress popular in Europe, c. 1735–50. Drawing by author from an English source, *Patterns of Fashion, I* by Janet Arnold.

ILL. 19. Drawing by author of 1736 trapeze-style dress from engraving (Fig. 229) in *History of Fashions*, by R. Pistolese and Ruth Horsting. Hairstyle, c. 1742, from a painting by John Smibert, Yale University Art Gallery.

ILL. 20. Drawing by author of a young woman's summer dress, from an illustration in *Deutsche Volkstrachten*, by Friedrich Hottenroth (Augsburg, Germany, p. 196), courtesy the Library of the Costume Institute, Metropolitan Museum of Art, New York, NY.

ILL. 21. Drawing by author from a china figurine, shepherdess costume. Nymphenburg southern Germany and Austria, c. 1750–65. From *A Pictorial History of Costume*, by Wolfgang Bruhn, Max Tilke, p. 112, Fig. 5. Courtesy Library of the Costume Institute, Metropolitan Museum of Art, New York, NY.

ILL. 22. Illustration by author. Coming out Bride quote from *The Sabbath in Puritan New England*, by Alice Morse Earle, 1891, 1969, pp. 233, 234.

ILL. 23. Pattern of the brocade of gold silk brocade wedding gown of Mary Leverett, who married Major John Dennison of Ipswich in 1719, in Cambridge, MA. Drawing by author.

ILL. 24. The style of the above dress, front view. Drawing by author.

ILL. 25. Style of the dress, back view. Drawing by author. The above gold silk brocade gown (1719) is found in the Essex Institute, Salem, MA; given by Mrs. William West.

ILL. 26. Artist's rendering in watercolor by Betty Fuerst. Found in the *Index of American Design*, National Gallery of Art, Washington, D.C. The gown is in the Bostonian Society, Old State House, Boston, MA.

CHAPTER 3

ILL. 27. Wedding gown of Esther Marvel, a New England Quaker, married in Salem, MA about 1750. Redrawn from illustration in *History of American Costume*, by Elisabeth McClellan, *Book I*, p. 166, Fig. 212 (drawing by author).

ILL. 28. Brown ribbed silk wedding dress, Quaker, worn by Sarah Newbold, who married Jonathan Barton in 1766 in Mansfield, NJ. In the photograph: the gray silk bonnet, c. 1850; the brown silk bag, probably owned by the daughter of Sarah Newbold, c. 1800. Gown is in the costume collection, Fashion Wing, Philadelphia Museum of Art, Philadelphia, PA. Given by Mrs. Francis Gummere and Mrs. Thomas F. Branson.

ILL. 29. Quaker wedding dress of tan taffeta worn by Margaret Shoemaker, who married Michael Newbold, October 4, 1798, in Philadelphia. Dress, bonnet, and accessories are in the costume collection, Fashion Wing, Philadelphia Museum of Art, Philadelphia, PA. Given by Mrs. Percival Parrish.

ILL. 30. White satin wedding dress of Mrs. St. Clair, married in 1760 in Philadelphia. From *Historic Dress in America, 1607–1800*, vol. 1, by Elisabeth McClellan (England: Benjamin Bloom, 1904). Artwork by author.

ILL. 31. Back view of the above dress. Artwork by author.

ILL. 32. Eighteen-inch French Fashion Lady. Gesland body, bisque head, hands, and lower legs, c. 1870. Photo by John Axe, Youngstown, Ohio. From the collection of Joyce Kintner, Pittsburgh, PA.

ILL. 33. Brocaded ivory taffeta trousseau dress with Watteau back, 1752. Courtesy Wadsworth Atheneum, Hartford, CT. Gift of Rev. and Mrs. Krumbhaar.

ILL. 34. Wedding gown worn about 1765 by Mrs. Mary (Lynde) Oliver, Salem, MA. The gown is in the Essex Institute, Salem, MA.

ILL. 35. Taupe silk brocade wedding dress, c. 1776. Gown is in the costume collection of the Brooklyn Museum, Dept. of Costumes and Textiles, Brooklyn, NY. Gift of Miss Edith C. Viele.

ILL. 36. Brocaded silk wedding gown, part of the trousseau worn by Mrs. George Sutton, married in Philadelphia in 1783. Gown is in the costume collection, Fashion Wing, Philadelphia Museum of Art. Given by Mrs. Catherine E. Dallett Smith and Mrs. Judith J. Dallett Budd.

ILL. 37. Wedding dress of fine hand-painted linen, worn by Miss Lucrece Carew of Norwich, CT. Dress and long satin cape in the Brooklyn Museum, Dept. of Costumes and Textiles. (Drawing by author.)

ILLS. 38, 39. Color details of the floral watercolor painting for border of the above dress. (Drawings by author.)

ILLS. 40, 41, 42, 43. Two-piece satin and mull (crêpe) wedding dress, worn by Eunice Hooper, who married her cousin, John Hooper, in Marblehead, MA, in 1799. Gown is in the costume collection of the Museum of Fine Arts, Boston, MA. Gift of Mrs. Ward Thoron.

ILL. 44. Painting entitled *Washington's Last Birthday* by H. A. Ogden in 1899. Reprinted courtesy of Woodlawn Plantation, Mount Vernon, VA. Property of the National Trust for Historic Preservation, Washington, D.C.

CHAPTER 4

ILL. 45. Wedding gown of white satin brocade with floral stripe, c. 1800. Gown is in the costume

collection, Fashion Wing, Philadelphia Museum of Art. Given by Mrs. Paul Reid Tait.

ILL. 46. White silk with small floral pattern, worn by Sarah MaClay (daughter of William MaClay, one of the first two senators from Pennsylvania, and granddaughter of John Harris, founder of Harrisburg) at her 1804 marriage to Maj. John Irwin. Gown is in the costume collection, Fashion Wing, Philadelphia Museum of Art. Given by L. Hazelton Mirkil in memory of Mary Carter Mirkil.

ILL. 47. Artist's rendering of 1812 wedding gown in the costume collection of the Museum of the City of New York, NY. It was worn by Katherine von Lengerke, who married George August Meyer. Donor: Mrs. Eliot Norton. Artwork by Gertrude Lemberg is in the National Gallery of Art, Washington, D.C., *Index of American Design.*

ILL. 48. Gray satin wedding dress worn by Lydia Poultney, who married James B. Thompson in 1809. Gown is in the costume collection, Fashion Wing, Philadelphia Museum of Art. Bequest of Lydia Thompson Morris.

ILL. 49. Sheer taffeta gown (1817), in the costume collection of the Brooklyn Museum, Dept. of Costumes and Textiles, Brooklyn, NY. (Drawing by author.)

ILL. 50. Empire-style gown of ivory silk twill (1812), in the Costume Institute, Metropolitan Museum of Art, New York City, NY. (Drawing by author.)

ILL. 51. Fashion plate from *The Repository of Arts, Literature, Commerce, Manufacturers, Fashion and Politics* (London: R. Ackermann, 1816), vol. 1, no. 6, plate 33. Reprinted courtesy of the Henry Francis duPont Winterthur Museum Library, Collection of Printed Books, Winterthur, DE.

ILL. 52. Fashion plate from *The Repository . . .* (London: R. Ackermann, 1818), p. 183, plate 16. Reprinted courtesy of the Henry Francis duPont Winterthur Museum Library, Collection of Printed Books.

CHAPTER 5

ILL. 53. Brown satin wedding dress of Mary Downing, who married George Valentine in Philadelphia, 1822. Privately owned by descendant in

Wilmington, DE. (Watercolor by author.)

ILL. 54. Back view of the above dress.

ILL. 55. White satin wedding gown of Miss Colquhoun of Petersburg, VA, married in 1824. Illustration found in *Historic Dress in America,* p. 139. Redrawn for this publication by author.

ILL. 56. White crêpe satin wedding dress (1825), in the Brooklyn Museum, Dept. of Costumes and Textiles, Brooklyn, NY. Artwork by author.

ILL. 57. English fashion plate, steel engraving, delicately colored. From *The Repository* . . . (London: R. Ackermann, January, 1, 1827), vol. 10, plate 14. Courtesy Henry Francis DuPont Winterthur Museum Library, DE.

ILL. 58. Watercolor by author of projected wedding dress (with satin spencer) of a wedding described in letter written by Emily G. Swift (Mrs. E. G.), February 13, 1829. Letter is in the Library RBR of the Winterthur Museum, Winterthur, DE.

ILL. 59. (Not a wedding dress.) Steel engraving portrait of Marie Caroline, Duchess of Berry (France), from *Ridpath's History of the World,* vol. 8, p. 488.

ILL. 60. Steel engraving, portrait of Queen Amalia (Germany), from *Ridpath's History of the World,* vol. 8, p. 726.

ILL. 61. Steel engraving, portrait of Mlle. Henrietta Sontag, Germany. Reproduced from the Collections of the Library of Congress, Washington, D.C.

ILL. 62. Ivory satin wedding gown, 1834, in the Philadelphia Museum of Art, Dept. of Costumes and Textiles. Given by Miss Francis McIlvaine.

ILL. 63. From French Fashion publication *Costumes de Modes,* October 1832, p. 241, plate 194. Courtesy Library of Henry Francis duPont Winterthur Museum, DE, collection of printed books.

ILL. 64. Watercolor by author, of wedding dress, c. 1837, found in the Montclair Art Museum, Montclair, NJ.

ILLS. 65, 66. White batiste blouse and light olive green silk skirt early 1830s, worn by Fannie Cushing King, of Indiana. Both blouse and skirt found in the costume collection, Texas Tech University Museum, Lubbock, TX. Artwork by author.

ILLS. 67–72. A 5-part wedding costume, 1831. Found in the Costume Institute, Metropolitan

Museum of Art, New York, NY. (Artwork by author.)

ILL. 67. Ivory satin wedding dress, complete with accessories.

ILL. 68. Ivory satin dress with edging detail.

ILL. 69. Separate underskirt of satin.

ILLS. 70, 71. Lace bertha collar of above dress.

ILL. 72. Cascade wreath, which was attached to the veil.

ILL. 73. Plum-colored silk wedding dress worn by Margaret (Peggy) Burnell, c. 1835. Dress is of New England origin. Artwork by author. From the Westerfield Collection in the Brooklyn Museum, Dept. of Costumes and Textiles, Brooklyn, NY.

ILL. 74. White silk dress of jacquard-woven taffeta, in a scattered floral pattern, worn by Sophia W. Olcott, who married John I. Brower on May 20, 1835. Artwork by author. Gown is in the Costume Institute, Metropolitan Museum of Art, New York, NY.

ILL. 75. Fabric detail of white sheer embroidered wedding dress worn by Ann Elizabeth Crittenden, who married Samuel David Gamble, August 15, 1837, in Collonensville, Monroe County, Georgia. Dress found in the Atlanta Historical Society, Atlanta, GA. Gift of Mrs. Frank Sheffield, Atlanta, GA. (Artwork by author.)

ILL. 76. Gold silk wedding dress worn by Jane Thompson who married Mr. Burkhead in 1837. Dress is in the Arizona Costume Institute, Phoenix Art Museum, Phoenix, AZ. Gift of Mrs. W. Smith Pickrell. (Artwork by author).

ILLS. 77–80. Pale gold fancy-weave silk damask dress of Juliette Learned, married on July 12, 1838, in Bangor, ME. Dress is in the Costume Institute, Metropolitan Museum of Art, NY. (Artwork by author.)

ILL. 81. White wedding dress of Frances Shippen, who married Edgar Huidekoper in 1838. Dress is in the Philadelphia Museum of Art. Gift of George Doane Wells.

ILL. 82. Dress of white challis with silk cross-barred design. Worn by Harriet Maria Spelman, who married Estes Howe on August 20, 1838. (Artwork by author.) Gown is in the Museum of Fine Arts, Boston, MA. Gift of Miss Lois Lilley Howe.

ILL. 83. Lithograph entitled *The Marriage* published by N. Currier, 1847. Reproduced from the Collections of the Library of Congress, Washington, D.C.

ILL. 84. Hand-colored steel engraving; print by J. Baillie (1846), entitled *The Young Bride*. Reproduced from the Collections of the Library of Congress.

ILL. 85. Wedding dress of net, worn by Maria Speir, who married Aaron Reid in 1844. Gown is in the Costume Collection of the Museum of the City of New York, NY.

ILL. 86. Leaf-figured satin gown of Susan Maria Coolidge, who married John Van Santnoord on March 21, 1844. Gown is in the Philadelphia Museum of Art. Given by Mr. Henry G. Beerits.

ILL. 87. Painting in full color, entitled *Die Tochter des Kunstlers* (the artist's daughter), Munich, Germany.

ILL. 88. Morning wedding dress of net worn by Elizabeth E. Furman, who married Josiah J. Allen on November 23, 1843. (Artwork by author.) Costume is in the Costume Institute, Metropolitan Museum of Art, New York, NY. Gift of Mrs. Clarkson Runyon.

ILL. 89. Ivory silk moiré dress with French Lille lace edging. Worn by Smeline Vose, who married Charles Cox, c. 1845. (Artwork by author.) Costume is in the Costume Institute, Metropolitan Museum of Art, New York, NY. Gift of Mrs. Osborne Howes.

ILL. 90. Steel engraving of Adelaide, the French Princess of Orleans. Print from *Ridpath's History of the World*, vol. 8, p. 498.

ILL. 91. Watercolor by author redrawn from a painting by W. Dendy Sadler entitled *For Weal or Woe*, a garden bridal reception (detail of bride only).

ILL. 92. Creamy white dress (artwork by author), worn by Julia Mary Weeks, who married Henry G. deForest on April 15, 1847. Dress, veil, wreath, and handkerchief in the Brooklyn Museum (Dept. of Costumes and Textiles), Brooklyn, NY.

ILLS. 93, 94. Satin gown of 1849, found in the Montclair Museum of Art, Montclair, NJ. Gift of Miss Ruth Trappan. Photograph by Edward Harvey.

ILLS. 95, 96. Creamy white organdy dress worn by Almira Sage at her wedding in 1849. (Artwork by author.) Gown is in the Costume Institute, Metropolitan Museum of Art, New York, NY. Gift of Mrs. Pierre S. DuPont III.

ILL. 97. Print from 1847 lithograph entitled *The Bride*. Reproduced from the Collections of the Library of Congress, Washington, DC.

ILL. 98. White silk taffeta wedding dress (1849), found in the Costume Institute, Metropolitan Museum of Art, New York, NY. (Artwork by author.)

CHAPTER 6

ILL. 99. Paisley shawl, in the trousseau of Sarah Maria Meigs, who was married in 1838. Utah Pioneer Costume Research Project #388, Special Collections. Courtesy University of Utah Library, Salt Lake City, UT.

ILL. 100. Paisley shawl in the trousseau of Mary Thorpe Beal, married in 1854. Utah Pioneer Costume Research Project #75, Special Collections. Courtesy University of Utah Library, Salt Lake City, UT.

ILL. 101. Cashmere plaid shawl, presented to Anniken J. Evanson on her wedding day, 1848, when she married Larsen Borresen. Utah Pioneer Research Project #104, Special Collections. Courtesy University of Utah Library, Salt Lake City, UT.

ILL. 102. An 1841 wedding dress, lavendar pinstripe on gray silk, worn by Anna Maria Wood, who married James Jones on January 13, 1841.

ILLS. 103, 104. Details of dress in Ill. 102. Utah Pioneer Costume Research Project #311, Special Collections. Courtesy University of Utah Library, Salt Lake City, UT.

ILL. 105. Lady's hood, from *Godey's Lady's Book and Magazine*, January 1860, p. 7.

ILL. 106. Wedding portrait of bride Lillie Marks of California, who married Joseph Goldtree in Tucson, AZ on June 29, 1879. Photograph courtesy of Arizona Historical Society, Tucson, AZ.

ILL. 107. White organdy wedding dress, worn by Caroline Knight Findley, who was married in 1878 at Santa Clara, UT. Utah Pioneer Costume Research Project #44, Special Collections. Courtesy University of Utah Library, Salt Lake City, UT.

Houston, TX., who married Dr. Robert T. Flewellen. Jacket is in the Harris County Heritage Society, Houston, TX. The bonnet is from a description in *Godey's Lady's Book,* 1860, p. 91. (Artwork by the author).

ILL. 135. The original wedding announcement. In the author's collection.

ILL. 136. All-black silk taffeta wedding dress. Worn by Hannah Weidensaul, who married John Rutherford in 1860. (Artwork by author) Gown is in the Arizona Costume Institute, Phoenix Art Museum, Phoenix, AZ. Gift of Mrs. H. W. Hitchcock.

ILL. 137. Complete bridal outfit, 1860; description of wedding costume from *Godey's Lady's Book and Magazine,* Steel Fashion Plate for January 1860, p. 91. (Artwork by Author).

ILL. 138. Silk taffeta and print stripe of watered moiré. Gown made and worn by Susanna E. Emminger, who married Jacob D. Daffensberger, October 18, 1860. Gown is in the William Penn Memorial Museum, Harrisburg, PA. Artwork by author.

ILL. 139. Back view of above dress.

ILL. 140. Shot-silk taffeta, blue and gold plaid wedding dress worn by Mary Booth of Alabama, who married Amos Jarmon Hughes on December 13, 1860. Dress is in the Atlanta Historical Society, Atlanta, GA. Gift of Mrs. C. Thomas Bruce.

ILL. 141. Six wedding dresses in the December 1861 *Godey's Lady's Book,* p. 543. Print courtesy of Dr. and Mrs. Jerry L. Case, Kennett Square, PA.

ILL. 142. Brown velvet wedding dress. Watercolor by Max Unger. Photograph courtesy of National Gallery of Art, Index of American Design, Washington, D.C.

ILL. 143. Purple taffeta wedding gown worn by Annie Horatia Jones (daughter of Judge John Richter Jones), who married Daniel Rogers in 1865. Gown is in the Philadelphia Museum of Art, Dept. of Costumes and Textiles. Given by Mrs. Laussat R. Rogers.

ILL. 144. Drawing by author from *Godey's Lady's Book,* June 1868, p. 563 (Fig. 2).

ILL. 145. Drawing by author from *Godey's Lady's Book,* December 1868.

ILL. 146. Brown taffeta wedding dress worn by Bridget Dwyer Breen (grandmother of Mrs. William C. Frierson), married in 1865 in Tus-

caloosa County, AL. Gown is in the University of Alabama, Dept. of Clothing, Textiles and Interior Design, Tuscaloosa, AL.

ILL. 147. Satin wedding dress and ball gown by Worth, 1865. Worn by Clara Howard, who married James Flower. Gown is in the Museum of the City of New York. Gift of Pierre Lorillard Barbey, Jr.

ILL. 148. Silk satin hooped gown of Eliza M. Huddy Fagan, married in 1864. Gown is in the Chester County Historical Society, West Chester, PA.

ILL. 149. Sheer ivory wool Quaker dress worn by Mary Maule, who married Barclay R. Leeds, Philadelphia, PA., in 1856. Gown is in the Philadelphia Museum of Art. Gift of Mrs. Harris Cooperman and Mrs. Everett Mendelsohn.

ILL. 150. Photograph by Edward Harvey of sheer cotton mull wedding dress, 1870. Gown is in the costume collection of the Montclair Museum of Art, Montclair, NJ. Gift of Mrs. Theodore Dorman.

CHAPTER 9

ILL. 151. Three-piece wedding dress of Tillie W. Rapelje, who married Van Brunt Magaw on November 2, 1870, in New Lots, Long Island, N.Y. Gown and accessories in the Brooklyn Museum, Dept. of Costumes and Textiles, Brooklyn, N.Y. Gift of Mrs. Charles Iseley.

ILL. 152. Front of above dress. (Artwork by author.)

ILLS. 153 & 154. Gown of beige brilliantine, late 1860s. Gown is in the costume collection of the Texas Tech University museum, Lubbock, TX. (Artwork by author.)

ILL. 155. Pale gray-blue taffeta wedding dress worn by Narcissa Avery, who married Frederick Allen Claflin in Boston on November 23, 1870. Gown is in the Museum of Fine Arts costume collection, Boston, MA. Gift of Dr. Edith Francis Claflin and Miss Charlotte Isabel Claflin. (Artwork by author.)

ILL. 156. Five-piece wedding dress of Mary Francis Cooke, who married George B. Warren on October 29, 1873, in the Congregational Church in Hyde Park, MA. Gown was made at Hogg, Brown and Taylor's, drygoods merchants of Boston. Gown is in the costume collection of the

Museum of Fine Arts, Boston, MA. Gift of Miss Elsie G. Warren. (Artwork by author.)

ILLS. 157–60. Two-piece bustle dress of cream faille worn by Margaret Loper Baird, who married George Fox in Philadelphia, PA, in 1875. The dress was purchased at the Accessory Shop, 1532 West Columbia Ave., Philadelphia, PA. It is privately owned by a descendent, in Wilmington, DE, and has been preserved in its original box. (Artwork by author.)

ILL. 161. Gold and pale green taffeta and damask gown worn by Ellen Speakman, who married Robert Howard John on November 26, 1879. Gown is in the costume collection of the Chester County Historical Society, West Chester, PA. Gift of Helen and Zillah Speakman.

ILL. 162. Three brides from *Harper's Bazar,* August 1870.

ILL. 163. Steel fashion plate from *Godey's Lady's Book,* December 1872. Print courtesy of Dr. and Mrs. Jerry L. Case, Kennett Square, PA.

ILL. 164. Steel fashion plate from *Godey's Lady's Book,* August 1876. Print courtesy of Dr. and Mrs. Jerry L. Case, Kennett Square, PA.

ILL. 165. Children with bride dolls. Illustration from *Harper's Bazar,* January 10, 1874.

ILLS. 166–170. Wedding outfit of Mrs. John Henry Maginnis (1870). Gown and accessories are in the costume collection of the Louisiana State Museum, Jackson Square, New Orleans, LA. Gift of Mrs. John W. Mackay. (Artwork by author.)

ILL. 171. Gray taffeta two-piece wedding dress of Mary Ellen Wanamaker, who was married on October 25, 1877. Gown is in the costume collection of the Philadelphia Museum of Art, Philadelphia, PA. Gift of Mr. and Mrs. Samuel Wanamaker Fales.

ILL. 172. Worth wedding gown (1878) of ivory and gold satin damask, worn by Annie Schermerhorn, who married John Innes Kane on December 12, 1878. Gown is in the costume collection of the Museum of the City of New York. Gift of Miss Fannie M. Cottenet.

ILL. 173. Two-piece white wool wedding dress worn by Annie Laurie White, who married Willis Bascom Parks at Villa Rica, Georgia, May 8, 1880. Gown is in the University of Alabama, Dept. of Clothing, Textiles and Interior Design, Tuscaloosa, AL. (Artwork by author.)

ILL. 174. Satin gown, worn by Caroline H. Crane, who married Edward Canfield Lyon on January 13, 1880. Gown is in the costume collection of the Montclair Art Museum, Montclair, NJ. Gift of Mrs. Edward C. Lyon. (Photograph by Edward Harvey.)

ILL. 175. Satin gown (1883). Gown is in the costume collection of the Montclair Art Museum, Montclair, NJ. Gift of Mrs. R. P. Barbour. (Photograph by Edward Harvey.)

ILL. 176. Blue satin brocade gown worn by Nellie Low Chase, who married Charles Louie Colton in Leonia, NY, on October 1, 1884. Gown is in the Wadsworth Atheneum, Hartford, CT. Gift of Miss Lucretia Colton.

ILL. 177. Satin wedding dress (c. 1885) made by Lanouette, New York and Paris. Courtesy of Wadsworth Atheneum, Hartford, CT. Gift of Mrs. C. Frederic Beach.

ILL. 178. Two-piece brown wedding suit worn by Amanda Delp, who married Isaiah Ruth in 1886 in Montgomery County, PA. Gown is privately owned. (Artwork by author.) Courtesy of the Mennonite Heritage Center, Souderton, PA.

ILLS. 179, 180. Two photographs of Mr. and Mrs. Carl Lemke, married in Wausau, WI in 1888. Courtesy of the Marathon County Historical Museum, Wausau, WI.

ILL. 181. Wedding portrait of Alice Jeannette Whaley, who married Henry Reddick Wells on October 25, 1887, at the Cotton Exposition of 1887. Photograph property of Atlanta Historical Society, Atlanta, GA.

ILL. 182. Wedding portrait of Juana Gonzales, who married James Benton Glover on October 10, 1888, in Tucson, AZ. Courtesy of the Arizona Historical Society, Tucson, AZ.

ILL. 183. Blue silk faille wedding costume worn by Hattie Napier, who married Thomas Shive on December 18, 1890, in Vernon, TX. Gown is in the costume collection of Texas Tech University museum, Lubbock, TX.

ILL. 184. Myrtle green wool wedding suit worn by Josephine Ray, who married Judge Fleetwood Rice on September 19, 1899. Gown is in the University of Alabama, Dept. of Clothing, Textiles and Interior Design, Tuscaloosa, AL. (Artwork by author.)

ILL. 185. Bride's traveling hat illustration, *Ladies' Home Journal,* October 15, 1910, p. 46.

ILLS. 186, 187. Satin gown of Josephine Freeman Rand, who married Elfric Drew Ingall on April 19, 1892. Gown is in the costume collection of the Montclair Art Museum, Montclair, NJ. (Artwork by author.)

ILL. 188. Wedding portrait of Nonie Louise Nichols, who married Leigh F. Brown, September 5, 1891, in Tioga, TX. Courtesy of the costume collection of Texas Tech University museum, Lubbock, TX.

ILL. 189. *Godey's Lady's Book,* January 1891. Crêpe de chine gown, entire front trimmed with bands of ostrich feathers. Artwork by author.

ILL. 190. *Harper's Bazar,* 1893, p. 243.

ILL. 191. Crinkled crêpe wedding dress worn by Helen Harrison Morris (daughter of Governor Luzen B. Morris), who married Arthur F. Hadley on June 30, 1891. Gown by Barretts of New York. Courtesy of the Wadsworth Atheneum, Hartford, CT. Gift of Mrs. Morris Hadley.

ILL. 192. Silk wedding dress of Emma Fink, who married Hal-Yates Maxon on September 10, 1896, in West Liberty, IA. Dress privately owned. (Artwork by author.)

ILL. 193. Wedding party photograph. The bride is Lillie Otting, who married Henry Maerki on August 29, 1896, in Austin, TX. Courtesy of Austin History Center, Travis County collection, Austin, TX.

ILL. 194. Wedding portrait of Ida Howell Cramer (c. 1896). Courtesy of the Atlanta Historical Society, Atlanta, GA.

ILL. 195. Ivory silk satin wedding gown worn by Lena M. Goos, who married Michael J. O'Neill on June 7, 1898. Gown is in the Chester County Historical Society, West Chester, PA. Gift of Marie E. O'Neill.

ILL. 196. Wedding bodice with Paris label; designed by Raudnitz, 1897. Gown is in the Arizona Costume Institute of the Phoenix Art Museum, Phoenix, AZ. Gift of Mrs. Theodore Grosvenor.

ILL. 197. "The Wedding March," 1897 (from a stereopticon slide). Courtesy of the Library of Congress, Special Collections.

ILL. 198. Wedding portrait of Nina Louise Abadie, St. Louis, who married Pierre Augusta Bremond on December 16, 1897. Courtesy of the Austin History Center, Travis County collection, Family Archives, Austin, TX.

ILL. 199. Silk wedding dress worn by Annie Gardner, Camp Hill, PA, who married Harry Selby Watson, Jr. on April 18, 1899, in East Lemoyne, PA. Gown is in the William Penn Memorial Museum costume collection, Harrisburg, PA. (Artwork by author.)

ILL. 200. Wedding portrait of Gussie Parkhurst, who married DeLos Lemuel Hill, June 7, 1899. Courtesy of the Atlanta Historical Society, Atlanta, GA.

CHAPTER 10

ILLS. 201, 202. Pale blue embroidered crêpe de chine gown worn by Nellie Ward Donnan of Austin, TX, who married Clarence Lincoln Test of Philadelphia on May 1, 1901, in Austin, TX. Photographs, newspaper accounts, album, wedding dress, complete trousseau, and the marriage certificate are in the Austin History Center, Travis County collection, Austin, TX.

ILL. 203. *Trau-Schein* (Marriage certificate) of Lillie Otting and Henry Maerki, in the Austin History Center, Travis County collection, Austin, TX.

ILL. 204. Marriage certificate of author's maternal grandparents. Bride is Mattie J. Dietz, who married Solomon S. Rupp in Cumberland County, PA, on August 23, 1887. Owned by author.

ILL. 205. Cover photograph, November 1900. Reprinted with permission of *Ladies' Home Journal.*

ILL. 206. Wedding gown, trousseau, and accessories of Louise Gueringue LaBoube, who married George Burton Booker, Wilmington, DE, on April 22, 1903, in Philadelphia, PA. Gown and accessories in author's collection, also the brief biography of bride and her parents. (Artwork by author.)

ILL. 207. Bridal photograph of Armida Felix, who married Manuel H. Amado on May 1, 1901, in Tucson, AZ. Photograph courtesy of Arizona Historical Society, Tucson, AZ.

ILL. 208. Satin wedding dress (early 1900s) with lily pattern embroidery. Gown is in the University of Alabama, Department of Clothing, Textiles, and Interior Design, Tuscaloosa, AL. Artwork by author.

ILL. 209. Gown made and worn by Iza Bernice Shelton, who married Dr. Abel Wilson Atwood on July 7, 1903 at the home of her parents, Brooklyn, NY. Gown is in the Brooklyn Museum, Dept. of Costumes and Textiles, Brooklyn, NY. Gift of Mrs. Wister H. Walke.

ILL. 210. Photograph, "The Bride's Prayer" (c. 1905). Reproduced from the Collections of the Library of Congress, Washington, D.C.

ILL. 211. Bridal portrait of Irene Susannah Beaumont, age eighteen, who married Ivan Allen, Sr. in 1907. Courtesy of the Atlanta Historical Society.

ILL. 212. Photograph, "Dressing the Bride" (c. 1906). Reproduced from the Collections of the Library of Congress, Washington, D.C.

ILL. 213. Gown of white batiste with lace panels (1908). Gown is in the Texas Fashion Collection, North Texas State University, Denton, TX. (Artwork by author.)

ILL. 214. Nineteen-inch Simon Halbig German bisque doll with ball-jointed body. Costumed by owner, Joyce Kintner, Pittsburgh, PA. Doll has won blue ribbons in regional and National Federation of Doll Clubs, 1981 and 1982. From the collection of Joyce Kintner. Photographs by John Axe, Youngstown, Ohio.

ILL. 215. Hun wedding party, Lykens, PA. Photograph postcard in author's collection.

ILL. 216. Wedding party (1910). Photograph courtesy of the Atlanta Historical Society, Atlanta, Ga.

ILL. 217. Satin gown with metallic threads and beads (1913) worn by Mrs. Avis Reed. Gown in the Arizona Costume Institute, the Phoenix Art Museum, Phoenix, AZ. Gift of Mrs. Avis Reed.

ILL. 218. Wedding dress of Sadie Radcliff McPhail, married in 1914. Courtesy of the Rockford Museum, Rockford, IL.

ILL. 219. Dress pattern, #8364 *Journal* pattern, May 1914, by Family Media, Inc. Reprinted with permission of the *Ladies' Home Journal.*

ILL. 220. Wedding portrait. The bride is Carmelita Peyron, who married Rafael Valenzuela in 1915. Courtesy of the Arizona Historical Society, Mexican Heritage Project, Tucson, AZ. Gift of Aurelia Peyron Araneta.

CHAPTER 11

ILL. 221. From French fashion publication *Costumes de Modes,* June 1832, plate 194. Courtesy of Li-

brary of the Henry Francis duPont Winterthur Museum, Collection of Printed Books, Winterthur, DE.

ILL. 222. Veils and hairstyles from French fashion plate: *La Mode Illustrée,* 1872, no. 24, Paris.

ILL. 223. Bridal portrait of Darlene Ann Clark, who married William C. Stimmel, Jr., on August 28, 1971, in Massena, NY.

ILL. 224. *Harper's Bazar,* March 7, 1896, p. 184.

ILL. 225. Bridal portrait of Jane Robinson Kiser. Courtesy of the Atlanta Historical Society, Atlanta, GA.

ILLS. 226, 227. Watercolors by Katherine Berkemeyer, Sellersville, PA, painted in May 1914. Courtesy of Mrs. Florence Wenhold, Ridge Road, Perkasie, PA.

ILL. 228. Velveteen bonnet-veil worn by Reuby Tom Rhodes, who married Arnold Maeker on August 29, 1948. Gown, bonnet, and trousseau in the costume collection, Texas Tech University museum, Lubbock, TX.

ILL. 229. Harriet Chivinski, who married Philip Eric Bretz on July 28, 1979, in Packer Memorial Chapel, Lehigh University, Bethlehem, PA.

CHAPTER 12

ILL. 230. Bum-roll. (Artwork by author).

ILL. 231. Linen chemise, from the trousseau of Sarah Maria Meigs, who was married in 1838. Special Collections, University of Utah Library, Salt Lake City, UT.

ILL. 232. Hoopskirt (1860). (Artwork by author.)

ILL. 233. Hoopskirts (1866) (Artwork by author.)

ILL. 234. *Harper's Bazar,* February 15, 1896, p. 132.

ILL. 235. Advertisement, back cover, *Ladies' Home Journal,* May 1900.

ILL. 236. Advertisement, *Ladies' Home Journal,* September 1901.

ILL. 237. Advertisement, *Ladies' Home Journal,* February 1900, p. 37.

ILL. 238. Bust bodice (c. 1900). Courtesy of the University of Alabama, Dept. of Clothing, Textiles and Interior Design, Tuscaloosa, AL.

ILL. 239. Wire hip pads and bustles. The Sears Roebuck & Co. catalogue, 1902.

ILL. 240. Skirt and waist holder. *Ladies' Home Journal,* 1902.

ILL. 241. Wedding portrait of Mrs. Edward Inman (1901). Courtesy of the Atlanta Historical Society, Atlanta, GA.

ILL. 242. Blue garter (1903). Costume collection, the University of Texas at Austin, Austin, TX. Artwork by author.

CHAPTER 13

ILL. 243. Midnight blue serge wedding suit (1915). Courtesy of the Texas Fashion Collection, North Texas State University, Denton, TX. Gift of Mrs. John B. Ray. (Artwork by author.)

ILL. 244. Wedding shoes worn with the suit in ill. 243. Photograph courtesy of the Texas Fashion Collection, North Texas State University, Denton, TX.

ILL. 245. Silk, satin, and lace wedding dress (1915). With the wedding dress is the headpiece, matching shoes, garter, and matching nightgown (negligee). Courtesy of the University of Texas at Austin, College of Fine Arts, Dept. of Drama and Costume, Austin, TX. Gift of Miss Gloria Jameson, Austin, TX. (Artwork by author.)

ILL. 246. Back detail and satin shoes of gown in ill. 245. (Artwork by author.)

ILL. 247. Bridal photo of Viola Cochran, who married Benejah Cooksey Duffie, November 22, 1916. Courtesy of the Harris County Heritage Society, Houston, TX.

ILL. 248. Worth silk wedding dress worn by Frances Morgan who married Paul Pennoyer on June 16, 1917. Courtesy of the Museum of the City of New York, costume collection, New York, NY. Gift of Mrs. Paul Pennoyer, Sr.

ILL. 249. Cover illustration, *Woman's World* magazine, June 1929. (Illustrator: Miriam Story Hurford.)

ILL. 250. Soft-ribbed satin-backed silk gown worn by Ruth Whitman, who married John G. Pennypacker on April 14, 1928. Courtesy of the Wadsworth Atheneum, Hartford, CT. Gift of Mr. and Mrs. John G. Pennypacker.

ILL. 251. Satin, lace, and chiffon dress (1925) with belt of beads and pearls, designed in medallions and swag. Dress is in the author's collection. (Artwork by author.)

ILL. 252. Satin and silk chiffon wedding dress (1925). Dress is in the Harris County Heritage Society, Houston, TX. (Artwork by author.)

ILLS. 253, 254. Pale pink wedding dress of pineapple fiber, woven and embroidered (c. 1900) in the Philippines. Dress designed and made by Henri Bendel, NY, in 1927. Courtesy of the Arizona Costume Institute, Phoenix Art Museum, Phoenix, AZ. Gift of Mrs. Neilson Brown.

ILL. 255. Ecru georgette gown worn by Antoinette Johnson, who married William Collins Matthews on June 17, 1925, in Atlanta, GA. Photograph courtesy of the Atlanta Historical Society, costume collection, Atlanta, GA. Gift of Mrs. William Collins Matthews.

ILL. 256. Paris-made satin-and-lace dress (1927) worn by Mrs. St. John Garwood for her summer wedding in Houston, TX. Gown is in the University of Texas at Austin, College of Fine Arts, Dept. of Drama and Costumes, Austin, TX. Gift of Mrs. St. John Garwood. (Artwork by author.)

ILL. 257. Satin wedding dress of Yolande DuBois (daughter of Dr. W.E.B. DuBois), who married Countee Cullen on April 9, 1928, in Atlanta, GA. Courtesy, the Atlanta Historical Society, Atlanta, GA.

ILL. 258. Ivory silk chiffon wedding dress worn by Theresa Katherine Botenni, who married Donald Allbright in 1927. Gown is in the Riverside Municipal Museum, Riverside, CA. Gift of Mr. Donald Allbright.

CHAPTER 14

ILL. 259. Wedding gown of Julia Lowry Block Jones, of Atlanta, GA, married in 1942. Courtesy of the Atlanta Historical Society, Atlanta, GA. Gown is privately owned.

ILL. 260. Marquisette gown worn by the author, Catherine Louise Shepley, who married the Rev. W. Russell Zimmerman on June 20, 1942, in Sellersville, PA. Gown in the author's collection.

ILL. 261. A Tennessee wedding, a staged tableau. Photograph courtesy of the Bettmann Archive, Inc.

ILL. 262. "How I Planned My Own Wedding," by Betty Allen, *Ladies' Home Journal,* March 1914, p. 24. Reprinted with permission of Family Media, Inc.

ILL. 263. Courtesy of Claire Dratch, Inc., Bethesda, MD. From the *Washington Star,* March 8, 1970.

ILL. 264. Peau de soie and silk taffeta gown worn by Grace Kelly of Philadelphia, who married Prince Rainier III of Monaco in April 1956, in Monaco. This historic gown is preserved in the Fashion Wing, Philadelphia Museum of Art, sponsored and maintained by the Fashion Group of Philadelphia. Given by Her Serene Highness, Princess Grace de Monaco. Photographed by the Philadelphia Museum of Art.

CHAPTER 15

ILL. 265. White lace gown worn by Tillie Cohen, who married Nathan Falk in 1933. Gown is privately owned by Mrs. Nathan Falk and Carolee Falk Jaspan. Photograph courtesy of Mrs. Nathan Falk and Riverside Municipal Museum, Riverside, CA.

ILL. 266. Ivory satin gown, bias cut with "trained" spencer, by Lanvin, Paris (1931). Wedding veil of net and rosepoint. Gown worn by Mrs. Henry Bemis. Gown is in the Arizona Costume Institute, Phoenix Art Museum, Phoenix, AZ. Gift of Mrs. Henry Bemis.

ILL. 267. All-lace gown (c. 1934). Gown and veil in author's collection. (Artwork by author.)

ILLS. 268, 269. Ecru georgette and lace dress worn by Jessie Larve Sawyer, who married Cye Tankersley on June 8, 1930, in Brownfield, TX. Dress is in the Texas Tech University museum, Lubbock, TX. Gift of Mrs. Larue Tankersley. (Artwork by author.)

ILL. 270. Photograph of bridal party. The bride is Margaret Sellers, who married Edwin W. Andrews on June 28, 1932, in Sellersville, PA. Photograph property of author.

ILL. 271. White knitted wedding dress of Mrs. Candace Bryant Smith, married in 1935. Dress and matching hat designed and made by the bride. Photograph courtesy of the Atlanta Historical Society, Atlanta, GA.

ILL. 272. McCall's pattern, which was the inspiration for the knitted dress in Ill. 271. Pattern is

in the Atlanta Historical Society.

ILLS. 273, 274. White organdy wedding dress (c. 1935). Gown courtesy of the Nutshell, costumers, Wilmington, DE. (Artwork by author.)

ILL. 275. Wedding dress design by Adrian for Jeanette MacDonald (1937). Drawing is in the Los Angeles County Museum of Art, Costume Collection, Los Angeles, CA.

ILL. 276. Cover illustration, *Ladies' Home Journal,* June 1938. Reprinted with permission of Family Media, Inc.

ILL. 277. Photograph (1943). Reproduced from the Collections of the Library of Congress, Washington, D.C.

ILL. 278. Bride, Anna Di Constanzo, leaving her home at 118 Mulberry St., NYC, on July 2, 1940. Photograph property of Culver Pictures, Inc., NY.

ILL. 279. Burgundy velvet street-length dress and hat worn by Vivian Young, who married Eugene Crowl in Mount Vernon, NY, on October 6, 1942. Gown privately owned. (Artwork by author.)

ILL. 280. Photograph of Jewish wedding (c. 1942). Photo property of Culver Pictures, Inc., NY.

ILLS. 281, 282. Two-piece gray velvet wedding suit worn by Joy Smith, who married Earl Hoerner on October 3, 1948, in the Gettysburg College chapel, Gettysburg, PA. (Artwork by author.)

ILL. 283. Blue velveteen dress worn by Reuby Tom Rhodes, who married Arnold Maeker on August 29, 1948 in Lubbock, TX. Gown is in the costume collection, Texas Tech University museum, Lubbock, TX.

CHAPTER 16

ILL. 284. Gown of cameo-tinted Italian silk (1952) specially designed by William Cahill of California for presentation to the Fashion Wing of the Philadelphia Museum of Art. Gift of Strawbridge and Clothier through the Philadelphia Fashion Group.

ILL. 285. Gown worn by Martha Jane Rupp, who married James Cooke on Orr's Island, ME, on August 30, 1952. Privately owned.

ILL. 286. Nylon net gown, skirt over crinoline hoop (1957). Privately owned.

ILL. 287. Street-length lace and taffeta gown (c.

1953), modeled by Lisa Lewis. Gown is in the author's collection. (Photo by Juniata Photo Service.)

ILL. 288. Gray lustrous silk, by designer James Galanos of California, and worn by Mrs. H. Michael Cline, married on February 16, 1955. Gown is in the Fashion Wing, Philadelphia Museum of Art. (Artwork by author.)

ILL. 289. Taffeta beaded gown. In the author's collection.

ILL. 290. White oyster satin gown in the fall 1959 collection of Tamara Yohanan of San Francisco, CA. Dress is in the costume collection, Los Angeles County Museum, Los Angeles, CA. (Artwork by author.)

ILL. 291. Lace detail of the dress in Ill. 290. (Artwork by author.)

CHAPTER 17

ILL. 292. Medieval-style wedding dress (A.D. 1300), worn by Susan Bean on December 31, 1983, Las Cruces, NM.

ILL. 293. Egyptian influence on wedding costume. Photograph property of Culver Pictures, Inc., NY.

ILL. 294. Photograph (1929) property of Culver Pictures, Inc., NY.

ILL. 295. Brocade caftan bridal gown. Courtesy of Toast and Strawberries, Washington, D.C.

ILL. 296. Tom Thumb wedding, by pupils of the Sellersville, PA, kindergarten, April 23, 1952. Photograph property of John H. Shepley.

ILL. 297. Wedding portrait of Lavinia Warren and General Tom Thumb. Photograph property of Culver Pictures, Inc., NY.

ILL. 298. Wedding party. The bride is Mattie Lindsay Poor, who married Marion P. Maus on June 28, 1899, at Skaneateles, NY. Photograph reproduced from the Collections of the Library of Congress, Washington, D.C.

ILL. 299. Fort Hamilton military wedding. The bride is Private Florence Sereguso, who married Sergeant John Queenland in April 1944. Photograph property of Culver Pictures, Inc., NY.

ILL. 300. Traditional West Point wedding. The bride is Yvonne C. Lewis, who married James A. Van Fleet, Jr. Photograph property of Culver Pictures, Inc., NY. (Photo by John Albert.)

CHAPTER 18

ILL. 301. White organdy wedding gown worn by Mary McFadden, who married Philip Victor Harari on September 25, 1964, in New York City. Gown is in the Costume Institute, Metropolitan Museum of Art, NY. Gift of Mary McFadden.

ILLS. 302, 303. Taffeta and lace miniskirt wedding dress from Bridal Originals, modeled by Marcie Lewis. Gown in the author's collection. (Photograph by Juniata Photo Service)

ILL. 304. Ivory silk moiré dress with hood (1968), by designer Gustave Tassell. Dress is in the costume collection, Fashion Wing, Philadelphia Museum of Art. (Artwork by author.) Gift of Mr. Gustave Tassell.

ILLS. 305, 306. White waffle-textured paper wedding dress (1967), designed by Anthony L. Muto of New York. Dress is in the costume collection, Fashion Wing, Philadelphia Museum of Art. It was shown at the Paper Couture Fashion Show at the Barclay Hotel and presented by the Fashion Group of Philadelphia on February 13, 1961. (Artwork by author.)

ILL. 307. Photograph of Qiana wedding dress. Courtesy of E. I. duPont de Nemours & Co., Textile Fibers Department.

ILL. 308. Crocheted orlon gown with hoop, worn by Nanette Smith (née Kennedy) of La Grange, IL. Courtesy of E. I. duPont de Nemours & Co.

ILL. 309. Ivory chiffon chemise (1920s style), by Barbara for Murray Hamburger. Courtesy Bride's magazine, copyright © 1973 by Condé Nast Publications, Inc.

ILL. 310. White peau de soie dress by Piccione. Courtesy Bride's magazine, copyright © 1973 by Conde Nast Publications, Inc.

ILL. 311. White silk albatross dress worn by Myrtle Maria Carpenter of Iowa, who married Ulysses Peter Nedrow of Nebraska on February 26, 1902, at Coon Rapids, IA. Photograph and gown privately owned.

ILL. 312. White mousseline de soie gown worn by Virginia Vine Fager, who married Richard Eugene Nedrow on June 11, 1949, in Ventura, CA. Gown privately owned.

ILL. 313. White peau d'ange gown, bicentennial

style, worn by Margaret Ann Nedrow, who married William Zures on December 2, 1972, in Placentia, CA. Gown privately owned.

ILL. 314. Cotton and polyester pinafore gown (1972) by Marion Moore. Courtesy *Bride's* magazine, copyright © 1972 by Condé Nast Publications, Inc. (Photograph by Stan Papich.)

ILL. 315. Brussels lace gown (1899), worn by Betsy Lamar, who married Sam Barrett. Privately owned by Jane Thomas Lamar (Mrs. Edward Lamar). Courtesy of Riverside Municipal Museum, Riverside, CA. (Photograph by Michael Perham.)

ILL. 316. Bridal robe of homespun worn by Lauren Kay of Wilmington, DE, who married Sigurd Anderson on September 27, 1974, at Rehoboth Beach, DE. Robe was designed and made by the bride; the printing, using textile block process, by Lois Kay, art teacher and artist.(Artwork by author.)

ILL. 317. Sheer floral print dress with lace (May 1977). Privately owned. (Artwork by author.)

ILL. 318. Gown with cathedral veil worn by Donna Marie Donegan, who married Nicholas A. Villanova on July 9, 1977, in Wilmington, DE. Gown privately owned. (Artwork by author.)

ILLS. 319, 320. Wedding ensemble designed and made by Pat Roth of Wilmington, DE. The dress has hand-embroidered crewel work on cuff and belt, using tapestry yarn in rainbow colors. Ensemble in collection of Pat Roth.

ILL. 321. Groom's white cotton overshirt with embroidered neck band. (Artwork by author.)

ILL. 322. White cotton peasant wedding dress from Mexico, worn by Holly Ann Schwenker, who married Craig Douglas Joyce on December 18, 1977 in New Hope, Bucks County, PA. Dress is privately owned. (Artwork by author.)

ILL. 323. Satin and chiffon wedding dress made and worn by Cheryl E. Emhardt, who married Robert W. Wallace, Jr., on August 20, 1977 in Wilmington, DE. Dress is privately owned.

ILL. 324. White silk-satin wedding gown designed by Janice Martin of Philadelphia, PA, for Marjorie Baum of New York, who was married on November 3, 1984, in Manchester, CT. (Photograph by Walter M. Faust.)

ILL. 325. White organza and silk schiffli embroidery gown worn by Lynda Gale Mathews, Belleville, PA, who married William James Long on September 1, 1984. Photo by Kim Yoder Photography.

Notes

1. Clinton A. Weslager. *The Delaware Indians: A History.* New Brunswick, NJ: Rutgers University Press, 1972, p. 52.

2. Captain John Smith. "The General Historie of Virginia, New-England and the Summer Isles." *Bibliotheca Americana.* Cleveland, OH: World Publishing Co., p. 12. The 1624 manuscript is in the Manuscript Library, Henry Francis DuPont Winterthur Museum Library, Rare Book Room, Winterthur, Delaware.

3. William Stith, "History of the First Discovery and Settlement of Virginia." *The History of American Costume, 1607–1870,* by Elisabeth McClellan. New York: Tudor Pub. Co., 1942.

4. Sarah Josepha Hale, "Providential: OR The First Wedding." *Godey's Lady's Book and Magazine,* 1852, p. 18. (Published monthly from 1830 to 1898 by Louis A. Godey, Publisher's Hall, 101 Chestnut Street, Philadelphia.)

5. Alice Morse Earle. *The Sabbath in Puritan New England.* Williamstown, MA: Corner House Publishers, 1969, p. 266.

6. Alice Morse Earle. *Two Centuries of Costume in America, 1620–1820.* New York: Dover, 1970, vol. 2, p. 601.

7. Kathleen Elgin. *The Quakers* (Freedom to Worship Series). New York: David McKay Co., 1968, p. 73.

8. Clinton A. Weslager. *Dutch Explorers, Traders, and Settlers in the Delaware Valley.* Philadelphia: University of Pennsylvania Press, 1961, p. 50.

9. A. D. Mellick. *The Story of an Old Farm.* Somerville, NJ: Unionist Gazette, 1889, p. 244.

10. Ibid. Quote by Professor Kalm, of Sweden, from the *Pennsylvania Gazette,* 1749.

11. Phebe H. Gibbons. *The Pennsylvania Dutch.* Philadelphia: J. B. Lippincott & Co., 1971, pp. 24, 28.

12. Vincent R. Tortora. "With Courtly Grace." *The Country Gentleman* (winter 1978), pp. 102–104.

13. Alice Morse Earle. *Two Centuries. . . ,* vol. 2, p. 633.

14. Ibid., p. 634.

15. Ann Monsarrat. *And the Bride Wore: The Story of the White Wedding.* New York: Dodd, Mead & Co., 1973, p. 79.

16. Amelia M. Gummere. *The Quaker: A Study in Costume.* Philadelphia: Ferris & Leach, 1901, p. 161.

17. Elizabeth Ann Evelyn and Dorothy Coleman. *The Age of Dolls.* Washington, D.C.: Dorothy S. Coleman, 1965, p. ii.

18. Amelia M. Gummere, *The Quaker,* p. 150.

19. Doris Langley Moore. *Fashion Through Fashion Plates, 1771–1970.* New York: Clarkson N. Potter, 1971, p. 11.

20. Gown in the Essex Institute, Salem, Massachusetts. The museum acknowledges the comment from Miss Janet Arnold of England, who said (on July 31, 1968) this could be an earlier fabric with eighteenth-century alterations.

21. Julius F. Sachse. "The German Pietists in Provincial Pennsylvania. *The History of American Costume, 1607–1870,* by Elisabeth McClellan, New York: Tudor Publishing Co., 1937, Book I, p. 130.

22. Ibid., p. 130.

23. *The Repository of Arts, Literature, Commerce, Manufacturers, Fashions and Politics,* vol. 1, no. 6 (June 1816). London: R. Ackermann.

24. Ann Monsarrat. *And the Bride Wore,* p. 113.

25. *Godey's Lady's Book and Magazine* (August 1849), p. 156.

26. Lillian Eichler. *The Customs of Mankind.* Garden City, NY: Doubleday, 1924, p. 275.

27. Alice Morse Earle. *Two Centuries. . . ,* vol 2, p. 643.

28. Norah Waugh. *The Cut of Women's Clothes.* New York: Theater Arts Books, 1968, p. 137.

29. Courtesy Library RBR, Manuscript Collection, Henry Francis DuPont Winterthur Museum, Winterthur, Delaware.

30. John Clark Ridpath. *Ridpath's History of the World.* Cincinnati, OH: Jones Brothers Pub. Co., 1916, vol. 7, p. 63.

31. Carolyn G. Bradley. *Western World Costume: An Outline History.* New York: Appleton-Century Crafts, 1954, p. 264.

32. Mary Austin. *Earth Horizon.* Boston: Houghton-Mifflin, 1932, p. 16.

33. Frank Marion Cockrell, "History of Early Dallas." (Originally published in weekly installments in the *Dallas Sunday News,* May 15, 1932, through August 28, 1932.) Permission to use material freely granted by George M. Dealey of the *Dallas News.* © summer 1944 by Monroe F. Cockrell. Page 10.

34. Kate B. Carter. *Heart Throbs of the West.* Salt Lake City, UT: Daughters of Utah Pioneers, 1948, vol. 8, p. 33.

35. Ibid., p. 40.

36. Utah Pioneer Costume Research Project #141, University of Utah Library, Salt Lake City, Utah.

37. Ibid.

38. Kate B. Carter. *Heart Throbs of the West,* vol. 8, p. 22.

39. Ibid., p. 22.

40. Ibid., p. 41.

41. Quoted from article by Beulah Burris McCallum. "Courage of 'Mother of Arizona' Left Deep Stamp on State" (June 9, 1956), Arizona Historical Society, Tucson, AZ. Appeared originally in the *Weekly Star,* Arizona, November 8, 1977.

42. Fischel and Von Boehn. *Modes and Manners of the Nineteenth Century.* Philadelphia: J. B. Lippincott, 1909, p. 57.

43. John Clark Ridpath. *Ridpath's History of the World,* vol. 8, p. 508.

44. "Chitchat Upon New York and Philadelphia Fashions for January." *Godey's Lady's Book and Magazine* (January 1860), p. 92.

45. Ibid., p. 91.

46. T. Wylie Davis. "The Prince of Wales Ball." *Our Town* (November 1961), p. 6. Published by the Museum of the City of New York.

47. Eliza Ripley. *Social Life in Old New Orleans.* New York: D. Appleton & Co., 1912, p. 267.

48. Dorothy Ford. "The Macy Parade on Thanksgiving Day." *Our Town* (November 1961), p. 5. A publication of the Museum of the City of New York.

49. *Dubuque Daily Herald,* December 8, 1874. Manuscript Collection, Henry Francis DuPont Winterthur Museum Library, Rare Book Room, Wintherthur, Delaware.

50. *Godey's Lady's Book and Magazine* (March 1896), p. 324; (June 1896), p. 659.

51. *San Diego Union,* December 30, 1890; February

18, 1891; April 2, 1891. The San Diego Historical Society, Padre Serra Museum Library, San Diego, California.

52. Mary E. Lewis and Dorothy Dignam. *The Marriage of Diamonds and Dolls*. New York: H. L. Lindquist Pub., 1947, p. 111.

53. Newspaper account on the Bremond family. Austin Public Library, Austin, Texas. Travis County Collection.

54. Mary E. Lewis and Dorothy Dignam. *The Marriage of Diamonds and Dolls,* p. 110.

55. *Ladies' Home Journal,* January 1914, p. 24.

56. Alice Morse Earle. *Two Centuries. . . ,* vol. 2, p. 639.

57. James Laver. *The Concise History of Costume and Fashion.* New York: Harry N. Abrams, 1969, p. 178.

58. Sears, Roebuck catalogue (1902), Chicago.

59. *Atlanta Journal* magazine section, November 26, 1933, p. 11. The Atlanta Historical Society Library, Atlanta, Georgia.

60. Viola Hermes Drath. "The Art Influence: What Fashion Owes Art." *National Observer* magazine section, October 30, 1967.

61. Mary E. Lewis and Dorothy Dignam. *The Marriage of Diamonds and Dolls,* p. 166.

62. "Milestones in the DuPont Company's Textile Fibers History." December 1980 (13th ed.), p. 1. Distributed by E. I. de Nemours & Co., Textile Fibers Department, Product Information Center, Wilmington, DE 19898.

63. *Britannica Book of the Year, 1956,* p. 748.

64. *Daily Texan* (University of Texas newspaper), March 7, 1977. Austin History Center, Travis County Collection, Austin Public Library, Austin, Texas.

65. "A Country Wedding." *Washington Star,* March 8, 1970, p. 8. "Brides," a Sunday Special.

66. W. Bruce Bell. "The Great and Only P. T. Barnum." *Readers Digest,* August 1981, p. 93.

67. William Perrine. "When Washington Was Married." *Ladies' Home Journal,* July 1899, p. 2.

68. *Philadelphia Inquirer,* "Today" magazine, July 16, 1972.